RESOURCE-FOCUSED THERAPY

Other titles in the
Systemic Thinking and Practice Series
edited by David Campbell & Ros Draper
published and distributed by Karnac Books

RESOURCE-FOCUSED
THERAPY

Wendel A. Ray
and
Bradford P. Keeney

Foreword by
Betty Alice Erickson

Systemic Thinking and Practice Series

Series Editors
David Campbell & Ros Draper

London
KARNAC BOOKS

Dedicated to John H. Weakland
... the therapeutic master of doing the most
with the least

This edition first published in 1993 by
H. Karnac (Books) Ltd.
58 Gloucester Road
London SW7 4QY

Copyright © 1993 by Wendel A. Ray and Bradford P. Keeney

The rights of Wendel A. Ray and Bradford P. Keeney to be identified as authors
of this work have been asserted in accordance with §§ 77 and 78 of the Copyright Design and Patents Act 1988.

British Library Cataloguing in Publication Data
Ray, Wendel A.
    Resource-Focused Therapy — (Systemic
    Thinking & Practice Series)
    I. Title   II. Keeney, Bradford P.
    III. Series
    616.89

    ISBN 1 85575 049 X

Printed in Great Britain by BPCC Wheatons Ltd, Exeter

CONTENTS

EDITORS' FOREWORD

As editors of this series, we are always looking for new ideas that will help carry the tide of systems thinking a bit further into the future. In doing so we have to be prepared to present ideas that challenge the basic assumptions of systemic approaches to family therapy. We had to decide when we considered this book, for example, whether to abandon some of our traditional distinctions between Strategic and Systemic approaches to family therapy. We decided this book must not be confined by our preconceptions. It is saying something new, and in order for therapists to be challenged by the material and to develop ideas of their own, they too will need to relinquish some traditional assumptions and read the book with a fresh, open mind.

This book invites the reader to see therapy in a different way. It is less about the interaction between therapist and family, more about the way the therapist defines problems. In the approach Ray and Keeney describe, family behaviour is uncoupled from a problem and turned into a resource for modelling new behaviour. They want to take the reader beyond the theoretical positions of *both* the problem-focused and the solution-focused therapies to a place where *all* family behaviour can be seen as resourceful. Seeing resourcefulness in behaviour leads to a new definition of therapy.

Therapists have dwelt recently on the use of self in family therapy, and this has proved a very helpful development, but this book charts a different course. It locates the therapist's mind "out there" in the real world of the family—their neighbours, their community, their hobbies, their dreams. The therapist attends to whatever the family is reaching for, and looks for resources in every context the family is in.

Ray and Keeney have worked together over a number of years to put their ideas into practice, and to teach others about their approach. As editors, we are pleased that they have reached a stage in their development where ideas have become so accessible to therapists. They have richly illustrated their thinking with carefully observed case material. This book not only lays bare their work for others to learn from, but the authors go one step further to describe training programmes for therapists who want to learn to use this approach.

David Campbell
Ros Draper

London
May 1993

FOREWORD

Betty Alice Erickson

Wendel Ray and Bradford Keeney have beautifully merged a sensible and practical approach with the creative atheoretical strategies of my father, the late Milton H. Erickson, M.D. What a pleasure to read state-of-the-art therapeutical methodology that so clearly carries forth the essence of Erickson's work.

Client resources are the means by which movement towards wise and productive realizations of healthy goals occurs. This is a premise that Erickson both believed and said. Ray and Keeney not only believe this, they say, write, and then show just that. They explain it in their theoretical framework, they demonstrate it in their case studies, and they teach it in their exercises.

So often, therapists think they have to "do something" for and to the client. Fifty years ago, Erickson was writing and teaching that the potential within can restore health and well-being. Today, Ray and Keeney teach clearly and precisely just how to elicit those assets in a framework that is uniquely their own. This concise paradigm is so clearly beneficial that the reader wonders why this logical and understandable approach has never before been articulated. Ray and Keeney take the reader step-by-step through their approach, and therapy becomes a voyage of enrichment for both the client and the therapist.

Resource-focused therapy is a context. Ray and Keeney avoid theoretical constructs except that whatever occurs can be a part of a resourceful context. Erickson believed strongly in the uniqueness of each person. He recognized that growth and health is fostered by the recognition, acceptance, and encouragement of individuality. By its very construction, resource-focused therapy respects individuality and cultivates respect.

Ray and Keeney understand therapy as a context full of resources instead of believing it to be actions aimed at resolving problems. Erickson knew this. Over and over he emphasized that whatever is presented should be used. He also knew that potentialities may not be fully realized. Part of the therapeutic process is the development of a favourable setting for growth of those capacities—exactly as Ray and Keeney explain.

The book ends with resource quotations from a variety of people. I will end with three from my father. "In brief, the behavior manifested by the subjects should be accepted and regarded as grist for the mill." "My learning over the years was that I tried to direct the patient too much. It took a long time [to learn] to let things develop and make use of things as they develop." And last, "You let the subject grow."

Milton H. Erickson Institute of Texas

ACKNOWLEDGEMENTS

Resource-focused therapy (RFT) is the product of a seven-year collaboration between the two authors. The clinical work and underlying theoretical orientation has been influenced by many people, both within and outside of the world of family therapy and brief therapy—individuals of renown and others less known, alive and deceased. A few to whom I feel particularly indebted are Don Jackson, Harry Stack Sullivan, Gregory Bateson, and Milton Erickson (through extensive reading and review of recordings, and enlightening discussions with people who knew and worked with them); John Weakland, Richard Fisch, Gianfranco Cecchin, William Saxon, Lynn Hoffman, Loren Bryant, Gerry Lane, and, of course, my co-author Brad Keeney. RFT is grounded in the work of these innovators.

During the past three years the refinement and testing out of these ideas in teaching and clinical practice has involved close collaboration with my colleague and friend R. Lamar Woodham, and a group of dedicated students and colleagues involved in the Resource-focused therapy Project: Mikal Fraizer, Dan Williams, Becki Biedenharn, Denise Morvant, Vaughn Bryant, David Hale,

Tom Moore, Doug Kline, Jackie Hand, Alice Crawford, Ken Parker, John Miller, Susan Cooley, Alan Demmit, and Pam Hansen.

And, finally, I want to express my deepest appreciation for my dearest Rayleen. Her unswerving encouragement and emotional support made completion of this work possible.

Wendel A. Ray

Resource-focused therapy began when I first met my colleague and co-author, Wendel Ray. This took place while he was a student in a doctoral program I directed at Texas Tech University. In our very first clinical case, the seeds were planted for the birth of RFT.

Since that time Wendel has become a leader in the field of family therapy. His historical work in studying the contributions of Don Jackson inspired the Jackson family to authorize Wendel to be Jackson's biographer. His recently published book with Gianfranco Cecchin and Gerry Lane, *Irreverence: A Strategy for Therapists' Survival*, has already established him as a cutting-edge voice for the field.

Wendel is the one responsible for building the context that enabled the evolution of RFT to take place. At his institution in Louisiana, we worked with clinical cases and spent long hours discussing with colleagues how to work more resourcefully with clients. I am most grateful to Wendel Ray's leadership in establishing RFT and to all his students and colleagues that I have had the pleasure of working with.

In addition, I want to acknowledge the therapists who have been directly helpful to me in my own development as a practitioner. These include Carl Whitaker, Ramon Corrales, Olga Silverstein, Luigi Boscolo, Gianfranco Cecchin, Jeffrey Ross, Charles Fishman, Sal Minuchin, Peggy Papp, Peggy Penn, Lynn Hoffman, Robert Shaw, Harold Goolishian, Monte Bobele, Harv Joanning, Connie Steele, William Quinn, Loren Bryant, Ron Chenail, Douglas Sprenkle, Cheryl Storm, and Tony Heath.

I am forever grateful to my son, Scott, for his dedication to imagination and play and to my wife, Mev Jenson, who inspires me to move forward on the journey.

Bradford P. Keeney

RESOURCE-FOCUSED THERAPY

CHAPTER ONE

Introduction

R esource-focused therapy (RFT) is a practical approach to working with people who complain of difficulties, dilemmas, impasses, and problems. It is based on paying the least amount of attention to problems that have become pathologized. RFT strictly focuses on bringing forth the natural resources of both clients and therapists. By "resource" is existentially meant *any* experience, belief, understanding, attitude, event, conduct, or interpersonal habit that contributes to the positive contextualization and realization of one's being. In its ideal form, RFT does not even appear as therapy; it aims to appear more as the performance of a conversation that engages both therapist and client in transforming their situation from one that is impoverishing to one that is resourceful.

RFT differs from most therapies in that it discounts the metaphor of *both* "therapist" and "client". We prefer seeing both parties as caught in the same dilemma: how can each be resource-ful to the other? What must the "client" say or perform to evoke a response from the "therapist" that will be resourceful to the "client"? What must the "therapist" say that evokes the "client" to evoke the "therapist"?

1

More simply put, what must take place to have conversation that is resourceful to all participants? Until the client says something that brings forth the creative imagination (and positive contributions) of the therapist, the therapist is in the situation of being treated by the client. Both therapist and client are problems until each is transformed—with the help of the other—and becomes resourceful, therapeutic, and healing to the situation.

Our focus is specifically on *resourceful contexts*. Whether an action, spoken word, or experience is resourceful is determined by the context embodying it. "Resourceful" does not refer to particular events, but to the context of events. A mother's praise for her child is not resourceful on the basis of the words alone, spoken in isolation. Praise is resourceful only when uttered in a context that both perceive as meaningful and positive.

Most of the knots that clients and therapists get themselves into stem from confusion generated by confounding the difference between context and the events being contextualized. A major contribution of Gregory Bateson (1972) was his noting over and over again how different levels of abstraction or understandings are often mixed up, breeding problematic configurations. "Crime is not the name of a simple action" was one of Bateson's favourite paradigmatic examples. The simple action of "shooting a gun" is not necessarily a crime. Crime is the name of a context of simple actions that may include "shooting a gun" or "hitting another person". Similarly, therapy is not the name of a single action. It is the name of a context of actions that often include "appearing at a scheduled time" and "paying a fee".

When the idea that therapy is a context and not a simple action is fully realized, a major shift in understanding takes place for the therapist. It then becomes clear that there are no particular right words, actions, or interventions that will necessarily work for a specific situation. What is called for is the movement of a problematic context into a resourceful context. In a resourceful context, all uttered lines and enacted conduct are contextualized, experienced, and realized as therapeutic.

Without a full commitment to recognizing the meaning of context, therapists will become confused by doing the right thing in the wrong context ("it doesn't work, but it should") or by doing the wrong thing in the right context ("it works, but it shouldn't").

However, with such a commitment, the paradigm of therapy is conceptually quite simple. It involves the transformation of the context within which client and therapist converse.

In the beginning of the theatrical play called "therapy", the opening context is often named "the problem". Act I, "the problem", finds a client stuck in the situation where his or her experience is contextualized as "problematic". When a therapist enters the client's problem context, the therapist participates in maintaining it. No matter what is said to the client, whether it be inquiring about the behavioural specifics of the problem, descriptions of attempted solutions, hypotheses about its origin, or professional categorizing and stigmatizing, if it contributes to the *theme of the problem* then the therapist is potentially helping the client stay stuck in a problem context.

In RFT, the goal of Act I is to get out of it and move into the next one, Act II. In most plays, the middle act is the transformational hinge, linking the beginning to the end. The final act, Act III, is for plays with resourceful endings, a situation of resolution and generativity. This is shown schematically in Figure 1. This diagram, the paradigm of a play, whether therapy or otherwise, is the simplest map available for understanding the structure of therapy.

With this map, therapy involves doing whatever is necessary to get out of the problem context. Again, anything said or done in the problem context, even if it seems the "right thing", is always a potential problem by virtue of its being contextualized as a member of the problematic context. *How* one gets out of this context is less important than getting out of it. Talking about the world series or fishing or cooking is usually more resourceful than discussing anxiety and depression. The trick, however, is eventually getting into a context where all that is discussed can be contextualized as a resource. Here, what was formerly called the "presenting problem" may now be discussed as a resource.

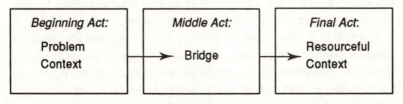

| Beginning Act: | Middle Act: | Final Act: |
| Problem Context | → Bridge | → Resourceful Context |

FIGURE 1

What is never to be forgotten is that therapy does not address problem particulars, but problem contexts. Problem behaviours are not the whole of the problem. The contextualization of any behaviour as a problem is the whole that embraces the problem. This orientation to therapy, previously presented in *Improvisational Therapy: A Practical Guide for Creative Clinical Strategies* (Keeney, 1991), is rooted entirely in keeping track of the context of one's performance.

In theatrical terms, the name of the scene in which one's lines are articulated must always be kept in mind. Offering help in a problematic or impoverished scene is often not helpful. Creating an opening that helps get you and the client out of impoverished contexts is the first step towards being therapeutic. Getting into and maintaining a constant presence in a resourceful context is the final act of therapy.

Resource-focused therapy is concerned with getting clients and therapists into a resourceful context as quickly and efficiently as possible. If it is possible to ignore the problem completely, this may be done. If the problem must be exaggerated to break into another scene, this may be encouraged.

Focusing on getting into and staying in a resourceful context requires minimizing other actions and understandings previously associated with the profession of therapy. In teaching RFT, trainees are encouraged to pretend that they are not therapists and that they have forgotten all their training, explanatory metaphors, and prescriptions for how to be professional. They are invited to be experimental performance artists, imaginative conversationalists, rhetorical consultants, or simply someone who uses and understands less professional understandings and acts more towards creating a context of resourceful experience.

Historically speaking, RFT is rooted in the genre of therapy called "Brief Therapy". Brief Therapy is rooted in Sullivan's "Interpersonal Theory" (1953) and was elaborated after his death by one of his students, Don D. Jackson. Sullivan was one of the first to insist that it makes no sense to talk of a self and its strivings separate from the interpersonal relations nexus of which it is part (Mullahy, 1967). First as a member of the Bateson research projects on paradox in communication (Bateson, Jackson, Haley, & Weakland, 1956; Jackson & Weakland, 1961), and later in the Conjoint

Family Therapy Model pioneered at the Mental Research Institute (MRI), which he founded in 1959, Jackson and his colleagues laid many of the foundations for Brief Therapy (Ray, 1992b). These pioneers did not work in isolation. They studied and were influenced by many of the leading therapists of their time, particularly the prodigious hypnotherapist Milton Erickson (Erickson, Haley, & Weakland, 1959; Haley, 1967).

The birth of one of the most influential brief therapy orientations was associated with the classic text written by three of Jackson's colleagues at the MRI—Paul Watzlawick, John Weakland, and Richard Fisch—entitled, *Change: Principles of Problem Formation and Problem Resolution* (1974). They abandoned much of the excessive weight of theoretical psychotherapy baggage to focus on problem definitions and descriptions of attempted solutions. As a therapeutic Occam's Razor, this orientation helped free many therapists to focus on designing imaginative interventions that aim at disrupting the interactional patterns embodying problem conduct.

In a similar vein, Jay Haley (another former member of Bateson's distinguished research team), in his classic contribution, *Problem-Solving Therapy* (1976), took specific aim at busting problems. Less parsimonious than Watzlawick, Weakland, and Fisch, Haley preferred a more elaborated mythology to account for the occurrence and persistence of symptoms. Influenced by his colleagues Minuchin and Montalvo, he developed a sociological map for contextualizing symptoms in terms of coalitions, hierarchy, and social power. To Haley's credit, a rigorous formal theory was never built. Instead his text loosely drew on simple heuristics and generalizations that aid the therapist in focusing in a specific way on alleviating "problem-in-social-sequences".

The potentially problematic catch in the work both of the Weakland, Fisch, and Watzlawick team and of Haley concerns their focus on the problem as the theme of therapy. Although their intention is to free the social system from being organized by a problem, their focus on the problem carries the risk that the therapist may contribute to maintaining presence in the problem context.

The work of de Shazer (1982, 1988), a student of Weakland, emphasizes solutions—the necessarily implied and complementary side of all problems. Here a de-emphasis is placed on problems per se and an effort is given to search for solution conduct. The potential problem with this approach is that a focus on solutions does not necessarily remove one from the problems they are supposed to solve.

To focus on either problems or solutions is to remain contextualized within the whole distinction of problems/solutions. The two are inseparable, and one side brings forth the other. As Fisch, Weakland, and Segal (1982) demonstrate, problems bring forth attempted solutions. Blocking the type of class or attempted solution is for them the efficient, although roundabout, way of alleviating the problem. For de Shazer and other solution-focused therapists, a focus on solutions brings forth—whether spoken about or not—problems. A potential disadvantage for both problem-focused and solution-focused therapies is that they each risk holding the theme of therapy in Act I, the context called "problem". In this context, both right and wrong solutions risk remaining a way of preserving the problem context.

Therapists who attempt to learn problem- and solution-focused therapies have too easily overlooked the context within which problems and solutions are discussed. These orientations tend to have a behavioristic feel to them that may seduce the therapist into looking at bits of action or sequences of action without regard to the context of rhetoric giving it meaning.

The contribution of the Milan approach to systemic family therapy, particularly the work of Cecchin and Boscolo (Boscolo, Cecchin, Hoffman, & Penn, 1987; Cecchin, Lane, & Ray, 1991, 1992, 1993), helped correct this deficiency in contextual vision. Their approach radically emphasizes the contexts of meaning (see Keeney & Ross, 1992). At the same time, being influenced by the theoretical ideas of coalitions, paradox, and so forth, this orientation also sets up the potential to fall into the trap of maintaining a focus on the problem/solution distinction, particularly with its focus on "the problem is the solution".

This reversal of the Watzlawick, Weakland, and Fisch slogan, "the solution is the problem", is half of the whole distinction: (the solution is the problem/the problem is the solution). Either side implies the other and maintains the whole theory of being in a universe of problems, solutions, problem solutions, and solution problems.

As part of this historical tradition of brief therapies, our work has naturally developed out of our understanding and practice of the contributions of Bateson, Sullivan, Jackson, Weakland, Fisch, Haley, Cecchin, and Boscolo, among others. What we bring to the theoretical table is an identification of what all these approaches seem to be after, in spite of the very different metaphors they use to discuss their understanding.

Specifically, the goal of therapy is to get clients and therapists out of problem/solution contexts and into a resourceful context. In a resourceful context the problem can be seen as a solution and solutions as problems. Here, however, the new understanding takes place outside of a problem/solution context.

PROBLEM-FOCUSED THERAPY

In illustrative terms, RFT evolved out of the history of brief therapy in the following fashion. Beginning with problem-focused therapies, the client's presenting complaints are moved to a specific problem focus and then taken towards trying new solutions. Here the final contextual theme is "problem solving", sometimes accompanied by the therapist's uncommon understanding that "solutions are often problems" (see Figure 2).

SOLUTION-FOCUSED THERAPY

Solution-focused therapies move the client's complaints to a solution focus and then go on to discuss the utilization of solution conduct as a practical means of resolving their problematic situation. Here the final contextual theme is "solving problems" with a

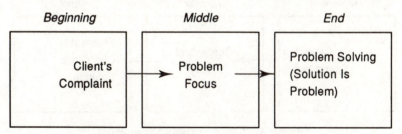

FIGURE 2   Problem-Focused Therapy

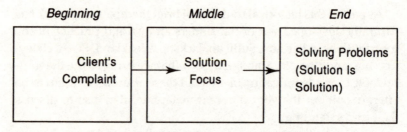

FIGURE 3   Solution-Focused Therapy

return to the common-sense understanding that "previously successful solutions may become re-solutions for other problems" (Figure 3).

MILAN SYSTEMIC THERAPY

The contextual or systemic orientation of Milan moves clients' complaints to the social contexts organizing their conduct. This eventually enables them to arrive at a place where problems are understood as contextual solutions (see Figure 4).

RESOURCE-FOCUSED THERAPY

Resource-focused therapy moves clients' presenting complaints towards *any* context that is simply more resourceful. It ends when a well-formed resourceful context is established wherein problems, solutions, and problem/solution contexts may be contextualized as resourceful. For RFT, resourceful themes are found to be more re-

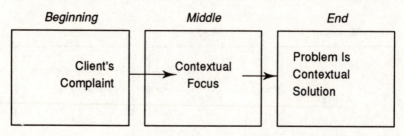

FIGURE 4   Milan Systemic Therapy

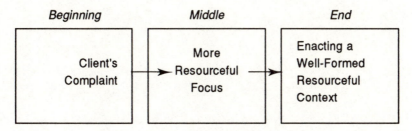

FIGURE 5   Resource-Focused Therapy

sourceful than problem, solution, or problem context themes (see Figure 5).

In RFT, therapy ideally ends up being outside of therapy. Therapy ends in a context of resourceful conduct, action that by its very definition does not require therapy. At the final stage, both the client and the therapist may be embarrassed to find themselves in therapy. As may be seen in the case studies that follow, clients and therapists enjoy and fully participate in bringing forth the breath of life and imagination within each other. In this healing context, there is no healer or therapist. All action in the healing context is healing for all participants.

* * *

In the chapters in this book, chapter two immediately presents the theoretical and procedural maps and anti-maps we have found useful in understanding RFT. Chapters three to six present case studies exemplifying the practice of RFT. Chapter seven is a set of exercises we have used to help therapists develop creative ways of bringing forth resourcefulness. The final chapter provides some resource quotes for resource-focused therapists.

CHAPTER TWO

Theoretical and procedural maps (and anti-maps)

Bradford P. Keeney & Wendel A. Ray

I n the first part of this chapter a delineation of theoretical ideas, notions, metaphors, heuristics, and maps is set forth that we find useful in understanding resource-focused therapy. We do not believe that a therapist necessarily needs to understand all of these or, indeed, any of them. It is possible to be a skilled practitioner of the approach without reference to any of these ideas. In our own experience with training others, however, these maps (and anti-maps) have often proved useful in the attempt to move therapists into the context of helping to build resourceful contexts.

The second part of the chapter sets out the practical procedures involved in conducting RFT. As will be seen, each session is conceived of as a play, composed of beginning, middle, and final acts.

A. *Theoretical maps (and anti-maps)*

1. Least amount of information:

RFT advises the bringing forth of the least information necessary from the client. This is particularly the case in Act I of therapy, in which the client attempts to explain his or her presence. The more information brought forth in a problem context, the more difficult it may be to get out of that problem context. Therapists should not forget that the more one asks, the more one gets. The data bank of the client is an infinite reservoir that includes contradictory, ever-changing descriptions and beliefs. Too many therapists drown in this vast sea of information. Once one finds something resourceful, use it. There may be no need to dig further.

2.   Least amount of time:

When the work is done, stop the session. How many times does a therapist create the therapeutic moment in the first 10 or 20 minutes of a session and then unwind it in the remaining time? When the session is over, recognize and utilize its closure. The idea that 40 to 60 minutes is required is less resourceful than creating well-formed sessions and closures.

3.   Single-session focus:

All sessions aim at being a whole therapy. This helps create a focus on achieving a beginning, middle, and end. Should the clients return for a subsequent session, that session is treated as a new case. Of course, this new case will have to consider the session that took place with that other therapist the time before. That other therapist, who might be you at another time, will have to be considered now as part of the therapy.

4.   Least amount of theory:

The less theoretical understanding in the mind of the therapist during a session, the more likely that the therapist can utilize his or her imagination. Theory is reserved for post-mortem analysis or late-night rap sessions. In the same way, a musician keeps conscious attention off music theory when performing. Theory has its place and contribution, but not necessarily in the mind of the therapist engaged with a client.

5.   Least is done:

Do as little as you have to in order to help move the conversation into a resourceful context. When it's there, leave it alone. If the client presents conduct that maintains the resourceful context, keep quiet. Not only should therapists do the least harm, they should *do the least*.

6. No psychology:

The professionalized rituals of thinking and treatment called psychology are avoided like the plague. No use of DSM-III is ever considered because it would be concretizing the problem context, making it extremely difficult to move therapy forward. Psychologizing—the use of hypotheses for explaining the internal and external workings of people—is also avoided; it keeps the focus off looking for resources and typically returns one to explaining non-resourceful conduct.

7. No sociology:

No hypotheses about social organizations are encouraged, for the same reasons given for abstaining from psychologizing. The sociological perspective too easily focuses or explains problems and de-focuses one from recognizing and utilizing resources.

8. No totalizing ideology:

Not only is there no emphasis given to psychology or sociology, but no ideology, whether modern, post-modern, narrative, or unspoken, is emphasized that distracts the therapist from the work at hand. Moving away from explaining problems and towards utilizing resources is the goal of RFT work.

9. No particular narrative:

No particular importance is given to ideologies and theories that emphasize stories and narratives. Clients are not seen as walking around with impoverished stories, nor are people in general seen as necessarily related to anything a theorist would call a story. This is not to say that stories are not used in RFT—if they are resourceful to a client, they may be used. The use of stories as a component of an ideology about stories in therapy is negated, whereas stories that are resourceful to clients are used.

10. Improvisation:

Therapists are improvisational to different degrees and in different ways. At the simplest level regarding particular utterances, no one ever really knows what lines will be spoken. Nevertheless, particular schools of therapy attempt to prescribe idealized conversations that clients and therapists should perform. In the schooled approaches to therapy, a therapist must wait for the client to say the right line. Problem-solving therapists, for example, have to wait for the client to define a problem before the conversation can move forward.

When a therapist does not follow a schema for therapeutic conversation, the degree of improvisation is further elaborated. Here, both therapist and client have no idea in the beginning where they will be going. Much of Milton Erickson's early clinical work (Haley, 1967) appeared this way, with a unique therapy built for each unique client and therapeutic situation.

RFT encourages an understanding and practice of the improvisational nature of therapeutic encounter. Like improvisational actors on a stage, a few lines are offered and a play must be created out of those lines. We never know what clients will present for us to work with. Our job is to join with them and create a play that moves the conversation into a final resourceful exit.

11. Radical constructivism/deconstructivism:

RFT aims to deconstruct problematic non-resourceful contexts and construct resourceful contexts. In this regard it is an attempt to build new realities for clients and therapists to enter and fully participate in. The path to building these realities requires acting differently in order to see and understand differently. Following Heinz von Foerster's (1984a, 1984b) inversion of cultural common sense, one must act in order to see. Therapists accustomed to first diagnosing and understanding before acting to attempt a change will find themselves working in reverse. Here the therapist acts first in order to understand how subsequently to act.

12. Cybernetic:

RFT is cybernetic in that outcomes, rather than hypotheses, shape the therapist's moves. Following the previous idea of action-based constructivism, the meaning of a behaviour is found in the subsequent behaviour it evokes, whether in oneself or in others (Jackson & Weakland, 1959; Jackson, 1965).

13. Systemic/contextual:

Again, the focus in RFT is on the context or system of uttered lines, action, and experience. The line, "I plan to kill myself", is less important than the context within which it is presented. A

RFT therapist would primarily think of how to change the context of the line rather than become organized by the line. If the therapist panics and reacts as if the client may kill himself, the therapist potentially contributes to the client's belief that this death threat is real. In this way the therapist may become an accessory to the crime by verifying and even escalating the validity of the impoverishing context.

Another therapist might ask whether the client has written a suicide note. How long will the note be? Typed or handwritten? What color ink? What about leaving a suicide book instead of a note? And so forth. Here the death threat is shifted into what initially appears to be one of the technicalities of the suicide note and finally, perhaps, to the context of writing.

The systemic/contextual view always places an importance on all relevant others who participate in building, creating, or destroying the client's realities. The emphasis will be restricted to utilizing other people in ways that contribute to maintaining a resourceful context.

14. Communicational process:

As was presented in a previous work (Keeney, 1991), therapy may be understood in terms of the conversational lines uttered by speakers, the frames that frame (contextualize) them, and the galleries that frame frames. This emphasis upon communicative performance encourages the use of theatrical metaphors to describe therapy. Other notions of communicational process elaborated elsewhere include orders of abstraction arranged in a recursive dialectical ladder (see Bateson, 1972; Keeney, 1983); and semantics, politics, change, stability, and meaningful noise (see Keeney & Silverstein, 1987; Keeney & Ross, 1992).

15. No official "narrator":

The therapist is not rigidly regarded as the sole director or editor of the conversational play. Because the therapist is kept in a state of ignorance due to limited information and blockage of professional explanation-making, the therapist provides a source of the random for the client. The ignorant therapist who is capable of speaking nonsense may help clients construct new ways of making sense of their lives.

RFT also rejects the idea that it is always useful for clients to *accept* the therapist's suggestions. All rejections of the therapist's ideas can be seen as resourceful: the rejections empower clients to take charge of the authorship and ownership of their participation.

The idea of a story implies a rigid literary form, beginning with "Once upon a time . . ." and ending with ". . . and they lived happily ever after". Most clients, however, do not organize their lives by any text that would be recognizable as the literary form of a story. If a therapist believes that such stories are there and should be there, then of course that therapist will aim to create them. We, however, assume that at best most people live in a collage of ever-changing, discontinuous strands of story lines that change and re-change given the particular social stage, time, and even the metabolism of the previous meal. Therapists addicted to the believed reality of stories may be replaying the theoretician's search for totalizing ideologies. The abstractions have simply been removed in favour of a more entertaining and manageable literary form.

16. Questions as interventions for change:

RFT turns the typical therapist's understanding of questions and interventions upside down. Questions are regarded as powerful interventions for change, namely change towards a different contextualization of the therapeutic conversation. We carefully design questions and provide observational time to note how clients respond to them.

17. Tasks and interventions as stabilizers:

Tasks, directives, and behavioural assignments, on the other hand, are seen as ways of prescribing action that keep the clients in the newly constructed therapeutic reality. Interventions do not aim to change; they are made to stabilize the contextual changes initiated by questions.

18. Therapy as theater: Play is the thing:

The emphasis on communicative performance, imagination, and improvisation encourages a spirit of play. The "smell of play" is one of the best indicators that one is in a resourceful context.

Where there is life, playfulness abounds, the absurd is legiti-
mized, and the experimental is welcomed.

B. *Clinical procedures*

1.   Act I: The set-up:

Resource-focused therapy regards a session as the creation of a
theatrical play. In this play of the therapeutic, three different acts
take place. Act I, the set-up, is the occasion for hearing the
presenting lines of the clients. The therapist may evoke these
lines in any fashion. What is most important is that the therapist
or team of observers identify any lines that may provide a hint or
direction towards a more resourceful contextualization of the
clients' talk.

Act I simply creates the building blocks, the setting of the
stage, the props, and the characters that will make up the
play. The subsequent acts move the conversation towards a
more resourceful context.

2.   Act II: Creating the resourceful context:

As soon as the therapist or therapy team begins to have a hunch
about how the conversation may be moved forward, a question
will be designed and delivered to the clients. Typically in a team
situation, a discussion and construction of this question takes
place behind the observing mirror. Often several lines given by
the clients in the set-up are tied together in a way that creates a
more general theme concerning how they are linked. This link-
age and the proposed theme (which may be from another client
line) is the basis for the question.

The resourceful theme, idea, explanation, suggestion, or
hunch is then dropped on the clients with instructions for them
to think and talk about it for a few minutes. The therapist may
then leave and watch their response from the observing room. If
the idea is accepted, the therapy moves forward. If it is rejected
or partially rejected, then the process is repeated and a discussion of the idea is listened to as if it were another Act I.

This approach does not create hypotheses—that is, possible
understandings of a situation. We prefer to create what Gerald
Rademeyer (personal communication 1992) calls a "diathesis",

defined as a disposition for organizing things in a certain way. Questions are a way of setting forth these diatheses or dispositions towards a more resourceful theme.

3.   Act III: Enacting the resourceful context:

Whereas *Act II* sets the stage for change by introducing the name of a therapeutic theme or context, *Act III* aims at stabilizing this change through prescribing action that only makes sense when done in the redefined situation. As the assignment is discussed, the client's lines are carefully woven into justifying, legitimizing, and fine-tuning the new understanding(s) brought about by the change in context of conversation.

All subsequent sessions begin with this same format—eliciting lines, usually from a follow-up to the previous assignment, further construction of the resourceful context, and additional enactments in the new reality.

* * *

In summary, *Act I* is where the clients bring the opening lines, typically understood as derived from an impoverished, often painful, context. *Act II* is the creation of new themes and *understandings* that are resourceful to both clients and therapists. And, finally, *Act III* is the prescription of *action* based on that resourceful understanding. Act II and Act III embody the two sides of therapeutic change—change in understanding and change in action, all based on the offerings given by the client in Act I.

In the case studies presented in chapters three to six, the structure of the case in terms of the current Act will be identified.

RFT requires the abandonment of building therapeutic towers of babel and practising one-upmanship games of political expertise over the client. It is an invitation for the therapist to learn to be more imaginative, more playful, more resourceful, and more human. As the therapist's humanity evolves, the appearance of therapy will diminish. What is left is a rebirth of occasions free from the straightjacket of prescribed templates, simplistic moralisms, and power games. Here the therapist abandons being a therapist in order to be more therapeutic. The absence of the therapeutic and the presence of resourceful creation is the goal of RFT. In its most complete form, RFT abandons its own ideals about being a school or orientation of therapy and instead moves into the territory of human beings joined together in the healing dance of living resourcefully with one another—one of the great mysteries which can never be fully spoken or known.

CHAPTER THREE

Worrying about the coach

A husband and wife, both police officers, were referred for therapy by a local therapist. The couple presented a variety of problems including complaints that they could not control their eight-year-old daughter, who had been diagnosed by a psychiatrist at a psychiatric institution as a "childhood schizo-phrenic". They also reported marital difficulties and the wife's depression, for which a psychiatrist prescribed Prozac.

In terms of family history, the maternal grandmother had asserted that nothing is wrong with the granddaughter. In mother's family, her brother had been described as the "perfect one". She often felt left out and never as included as her brother in her family of origin. Her father, a football coach, once had a perfect season and her mother and brother presented him with a plaque saying, "To the Best Coach in the World From Your Caring Wife and Son." She was not a part of this family episode. It was discovered that at present her father was having a losing football season.

In the following session, the therapist starts out by asking the couple to review what brought them into therapy, for the benefit of the consulting team. This sets up Act I, in which the clients put forth the presenting lines.

Throughout the first case the following abbreviations will be used:

TH = Therapist,   CN = Consultant
W = Wanda, wife   H = Hal, husband
C = Connie, daughter

ACT I: THE SET-UP

TH: Well, for the benefit of the team would you give a quick review of what brought you into therapy to begin with? Just a synopsis.

W: Gosh, it's been so long now.

H: Well, mainly we came because we were—our marriage was in some stress. And uh, she wanted us to seek some kind of counseling and I agreed to it because, you know, I felt like . . . and uh, so, I agreed to it at the time, but I told her, financially, we couldn't, we didn't know if we could afford it, but I don't know how she came across . . .

W: Alice, out at the hospital.

H: Oh, yeah, Alice told us . . .

W: She told us that we could . . .

TH: Your daughter was out at a psychiatric hospital one time?

W: Right.

H: Yeah.

W: All of this was kind of brought to a head while Connie was out in the hospital, and the stress of that just kind of brought everything to a head, dealing with that, you know, it just kind of brought everything else out more.

TH: Okay, okay. So it was two things, you guys were having trouble with the marriage and your daughter was having trouble.

W: And I really wasn't dealing with that very well either.

TH: I see.

W: You know?

TH: Now . . . it's been 2½ weeks since we met the last time?

H: No, about a week and a half.

TH: Week and a half. I still can't keep up with the time. Well, since then . . . how have things been going?

W: We've been getting along okay, as far as that goes. As far as our life in general, we're so broke that we're bored out of our minds, that's kind of getting to us. We can't go out and do anything and so we're homebound, pretty much. Now, I have noticed, and I was telling him about this last night and I don't know if it's just hormonal—because it's about that time—but, even taking this Prozac that I've been on for the past three weeks, I have felt twinges of depression the last few days. I mean, I could just feel that it was there and I just know that if I wasn't on this medication, I would just be bad off right now. I mean, it hasn't been, I've just barely felt kind of the confusion, the . . . I don't know, I could just tell it was there. It hasn't been anything that affected us, but I just could feel it. Other than that, we've been communicating and getting along pretty good.

TH: You got onto Prozac about three weeks ago?

W: Yeah, it was getting where this depression was not only affecting me at home, but it was causing me some problems at work and that's where I really put my foot down and said I've got to do something. It's bad enough at home, but when it also bleeds over into work, I couldn't do that.

TH: The depression, what's happening that . . .

W: I've been going through this for months and months and months.

TH: In relation to what, do you think?

W: I really don't know what because I was thinking about it one time and I remember a year ago, over a year ago, because I had my surgery, it was a year on September 28, and I remember kind of having, not necessarily the deep depression, but having a lot of the same confused feelings and . . . I've always had a terrible weight problem and I went up to Little Rock last year. I was 110 pounds overweight, at this time, and had "the" surgery, and it corrected that problem.

TH: Oh, I see. I understand.

W: Finally, after years of agony, but yeah, yeah. Get back on track here.

TH: Uh, you know, we were thinking, the team, we looked at the film. The . . . and we . . . and I wasn't aware, actually that you were having depression problems.

W: Oh, yeah.

Comment: Act I, the set-up with the clients' presenting lines has been reviewed. They are as follows:

• Marital stress
• Daughter has been in psychiatric hospital
• Couple is financially broke
• Bored and homebound
• Wife is taking Prozac for depression
• Wife confused
• Problems at work
• History of weight problem

Notice that the lines merely have been presented and therapy has avoided accepting and amplifying *any* of these impoverishing lines as a major theme. At this moment the therapist will begin looking for a way to introduce a resourceful line as a means of entering Act II.

ACT II: CREATING THE RESOURCEFUL CONTEXT

TH: . . . until now. But that just kind of makes sense in some ways, because when you think about it, with everything we've talked about so far, with the pull between you and mom, then the troubles you've been having with your daughter, and in all of that, you can imagine her behaviour and so forth, and the distress that the two of you have had in your marriage, just in the last year, uh, it uh . . . that the depression kind of makes sense.

In the team, we got to talking about the idea that there's one other person in your family that we're somewhat concerned about, other than you and your daughter, and uh . . . and that is your Dad. We got to talking about your Dad. You know, we got to talking about the fact that he's been having some real hard years at school, his teams' have been having bad years in football.

Comment: The therapist begins by stating the clients' presenting lines—troubles with daughter, marital distress, depression, troubles with parents. He then collapses these lines as belonging to the more major theme of "family concern". Using this theme as a transforma-tional hinge, the therapist shifts attention from the impoverished presenting lines towards concern for Wanda's father. This is done to set up a possibility of encouraging the family to move towards becoming resourceful to this father. In this way a seed is planted for the creation of a resourceful context. The therapy team, of course, has no way of knowing at this point whether this seed will take root.

W: It has been rough on him the last few years.

Comment: The seed for developing the resourceful context is begin-ning to germinate.

TH: What part of your depression is worry about your Dad? Because, you know, the kind of work he's in is one of the hardest . . .

Comment: The therapist is using an impoverished line from Act I— that is, reference to depression—as a way to continue reinforcing the resourceful theme of concern for Dad.

W: I worry about him, I really do.
TH: Well, coaching is one of the most stressful jobs known.
W: Well, because right now, he just turned 60 this year, and there's no hope of retirement in sight because of finances, and con-sidering how bad it's been the last few years, and he's—phys-ically, he's just not in as good a shape as he used to be. I mean,

he's never been physically good, like going out and jogging kind of shape, since he got out of playing college football. He's overweight, he's a smoker, drinks coffee, I mean, he's got all the bad habits, and every time I go to a ball game, I sit there and visualize him dropping on the sidelines with a heart attack and I'm . . . You know what I visualize? Going down there to do CPR on him. Every time I go to a game, that's exactly what goes through my mind. Because I feel it's going to happen one day. I really do.

Comment: The couple has accepted the new theme of concern over her Dad. They are no longer talking about their own problems but have changed their focus to discuss Dad's situation. The therapy will now step back and allow them to continue setting forth lines that keep them in Act II, the middle act of emphasizing concern over her Dad.

TH: Well, this leads to another question. It's kind of a natural thing to ask when we were talking about your father, if you weren't worried about him, I'd worry. I assume your mother worries about him?

W: Yeah, I think she does, yeah.

TH: If somehow, just . . . I can imagine this and I think it's going to happen pretty soon, if your daughter's behaviour was no longer a problem and magically she was no longer an issue to bring you in to talk with us, what . . .

Comment: The team telephone and suggest that the therapist keeps the focus on Dad.

TH: Would there be any problem to bring you back to talk to us?

W: Oh yeah.

TH: Tell me about it.

W: Well, me personally, I've always needed and wanted counseling. I've had a little bit here and there, and I've always know that . . .

Comment: The consultant working behind the mirror enters the therapy room.

CN: Hi, I'm Brad Keeney.

W: I'm Wanda.

CN: Hi, nice to meet you. We just think back there that this indeed is the most significant thing happening in the family. Our concern has been focused on your Dad and the particular life situation that he's in is uh . . . the kind of stress that being a football coach brings. And having been a successful coach and now to face not a season, but several seasons of failure and being in the health that he's in, I mean coaches don't have the longest lifespans for people.

Comment: The consultant's remarks are made solely to emphasize a focus on the theme of "concern for Dad".

W: Kind of like police officers.

CN: Precisely. Yeah, so we, uh . . . I think we need to talk about this as a group and you can perhaps just think about that . . .

W: Sounds good. This is fascinating. Yeah, this is fascinating to me though just how everything is . . .

TH: Connected?

W: Yeah, exactly.

Comment: At this time, the therapist and consultant leave the room. The couple will be observed to see if they stay in Act II, the new theme of focusing on Dad. The couple will be allowed to talk, as long as it is on this theme. The more they talk about Wanda's Dad, the more they are rooted in Act II (and uprooted from the presenting scene). Notice that their discussion while the therapist is away continues to maintain their presence in the new theme:

H: Well, I'm going to tell you what I think about football coaches in general. I know how I used to feel when I played football and, you know, you get psyched up for a game and especially if it's a close game where you're either down a touchdown or down a few points and the teams are to the point where you can go one way or the other, you know, you can score and break it open and win, especially when you get down to the final. ... I remember one game we got down to the final minute and a half, and we were down by three, we were three points down—a field goal down and we got the ball back and moved it right down the field and got to the ten and I felt like that, right then, if somebody would have touched me the wrong way or something, I would have blown up. I mean not mad, but just exploded. I was just so tense, you know, and everything's got to be right. Everybody's got to be thinking the same thing. That their job's got to be done just right. And just think, now I went through that once. But just think, coaches go through that year after year ...

W: He's been doing this for 35 years.

H: ... especially if they play games that are close, or the poor season he's having now. But he won last night.

W: Did he?

H: Yeah, 34–20. I tried to call him today and tell him congratulations.

W: I'll have to call him tonight.

H: But I ...

W: I know he's relieved. I kept thinking, Gosh, he's going to have a longer losing streak than he's ever had before.

H: No, he won, 34–20. I tried to call him this morning, but they weren't home.

W: See, the thing that was strange to me, all my life, after every football game, Thursday nights, Friday nights, in town, out of town, it wouldn't matter, we'd get to the house and I can always remember this, because like being in high school, growing up, the whole time I'm in school, we'd go out and always have food after the ball game because Daddy's going to be up for hours. And he comes in and he talks and talks and talks. "Did you see so and so do this? Well, he should have done that." Sitting there, you're going, "Yeah, uh-huh, yeah". You know, because I understand a lot of what was going on, but I mean, he'd go, you know, he'd talk about the intricacies of, you know, Joe Blow #63, should have turned left and he turned right and you're going, "Yeah, okay". But this would go on until two or three o'clock in the morning. We wouldn't all necessarily stay up with him, but I mean, you know, we would . . . people would come over a lot of times, I mean years ago, but now, the other night, he came home, he doesn't hardly talk about it anymore. You know, he'll talk a little bit. It's been so bad, I guess he just wants to put it out of his mind, I guess. But, when he came home the other night and he didn't even really want to sit and talk about it and I said, "Mother said something about wanting to go to the hot tub" that night, and I'm just thinking about him in terms of how he used to be all wound up for hours, you know, and I said, "You ought to go. It might help you sleep better". And he just shook his head and said, "I don't have any problem going to sleep anymore after a ball game". And that was weird.

H: Well, you know how I felt last night listening to a football game on the radio.

W: Yeah, I know.

H: See, I still get that tense feeling. Of course, I didn't get tense after the first three minutes, I got disgusted.

W: I guess if I hadn't left and I had been around here all this time and I had been either following Dad close, or following the other local high school teams all the time, you know, where I really stayed up on everything and kept up with who was playing and stuff, and what they were doing, I might still really get into it, but I don't get into it as much anymore.

Comment: Once a seed has been planted it is important to allow it to take root. This is a critical moment. Too short a discussion may allow the client to drift back into discussion of problems. Too long, and they might bankrupt it by drifting. The couple is firmly set in Act II and the therapy will now move to Act III. The therapist reenters the room. A task will be assigned for family action that only makes sense when viewed within the new understanding set forth in Act II. The team has designed an intervention based upon client lines that are aimed at bringing forth the family's resourcefulness in the theme of addressing concern for Dad.

ACT III: PRESCRIPTION FOR ENACTING
THE RESOURCEFUL CONTEXT

W: I can't believe that we're getting all this attention.

TH: We are really impressed by the seriousness of the situation. Given everything that is involved—your daughter's difficulties, how that is involved with everything going on with you and your Mom, and her and her Mom and your uncle Henry . . . with all of these complicated aspects of your situation—it strikes us that one of the most pressing things is your dad. You know how stressful his job of being coach is, and then there is the stress of the relationship between him and uncle Henry— how he has been put in an untenable situation there. That he's 60 years old, smokes and drinks coffee all the time. Your fear for his health, which is probably very legitimate. Based on this, we think that before anything else there is something we would like you to do, not only for you and your daughter, but for your whole family. Wanda, we want you to be in charge of this because you're the key person. We want you to go out and a buy a football and . . .

Comment: The therapist walks the family through the whole previous course of therapy, starting with an introduction of the presenting lines and proceeding through the shift to concern with grandfather. An intervention involving the theme of football is then introduced as something that could be helpful for the whole family. As will be seen, the metaphor of football enables the grandfather, the football coach, to be more clearly connected to the other members of the family team. The family, particularly the wife, nodded their heads in agreement and affirmation as the assignment was given.

W: Okay

TH: . . . after buying a football I want you to . . . do you have a movie camera? A home video camera? Or could you borrow one?

W: We can find one, I'm sure.

TH: Borrow a video camera, and then, without your father know-ing about it, involve your mother. You should probably ex-clude your brother. We want you to find a park somewhere and have a family football game, your father is not to know about it. Involve your mother. You'll need to decide who's going to be the coach. Don't involve her in buying the ball. You three go and buy the ball and then you orchestrate play-ing the family football game in secret without your father knowing about it. Decide who's going to play which position, who is going to be the star runner, and so forth. Work together to develop a number of plays that you can run. Film all of this with the camera. You are probably going to need a tripod or a friend to operate the camera. And we want you to come up with an imaginary opponent. Your daughter is going to be the star runner, right? Videotape the game, and then, after it is all over, we want you to sign the winning team ball, because you're obviously going to win the game, right? After all of you sign the ball, take it and the videotape to your Dad as a gift.

Comment: The football task clearly prescribes many kinds of poten-tially resourceful interactions. Football becomes the context within which the family may experience one another in resourceful ways.

W: That sounds neat!

H: Yes it does.

TH: I'm going to go back and talk to the team for a moment, but we think that doing something for your dad is really important right now.

Comment: At this point, the therapist leaves the therapy room to consult with the team. Note in the following how the couple's conversation, in the absence of the therapist, is already enacting the resourceful context. On their own, the intervention is further elaborated and resourceful interactions are described. In contrast to

the restricted behaviour exhibited by the family at the beginning of
therapy, when all they focused on was the problems they were ex-
periencing, the family is now unquestionably exhibiting coopera-
tion, optimism, and specific plans for carrying out the task.

W: I think he [her father] will get a real big kick out of that.

H: Yeah, he would. That would be neat.

W: Yep, and you know what would be funny is getting mamma to
      be the coach because she's always trying to tell him what he
      needs to be doing, so this time she can do it. That would be
      hilarious. Yep.

H: Yeah, and we can do it at the park near our house.

W: Yes we could do it there. Who do we know that has a camera?
      I know Cindy's got one. She would probably do it.

H: Okay.

W: Yeah. Connie could be the star runner. And uh, we have got to
      get a ball small enough for her to hold onto.

H: And you could be the quarterback [the lead member of team
      who decides which plays to run and who handles the ball].

W: Yes I think I should be the quarterback.

H: And uh, your mamma could be the coach.

W: Mamma's got to be the coach.

H: And your grandma could be the star receiver [the player to
      whom the football is thrown].

W: Right. Grandma's going to be in this. Just our immediate fam-
      ily. Yeah, send grandmother out on a long pass play.

H: As Bill Cosby says—Go down to the water tower and take a
      left or right. Look at me, I said left or right, and it should have
      been left and right.

W: (Laughing) If you say so.

H: I don't know my left from my right.

W: We will plan the game for the next time mother comes into
      town. I can get Cindy to do the filming.

H: Yeah, we need to buy a tape.

W: We can do it. It'll work.

H: We can set it up for next Sunday.

W: We may have to do it in the middle of the week because he says we need to do it soon.

H: Oh, okay.

W: We need to do it as soon as we can. I will get a hold of Mamma tonight and see when she can come down here to do it, or if she can't come down here we could go up there. But then, it would be real hard to get that camcorder from daddy without him asking why. So getting her to come down here is going to be the best thing.

H: Well (very long pause) . . . I could take some time off one day.

W: But if we get Cindy to film it, she doesn't get off until about 4:30, so let's just see when we can get Mamma to come down and see if we can get Cindy to do it for us, and then work from there.

H: And we'd have to do it quick then so we wouldn't run out of daylight.

W: Uh-huh.

H: That's neat.

W: And sign the game ball—I like that. We'll have to find a ball. If we got a Nerf football it'll be hard to sign.

H: No, not if you got one of those black pens that I've got, those felt-tip like pens . . .

W: Oh yea! O.K. Do you think Connie would be able to sign her name on it?

H: Yes. We will probably need to give her a whole side of the football to do it but . . .

W: We will let her sign it first and then work around it.

H: Yeah, we can work around her name. I think that would be pretty good.

W: Dad is really going to get a kick out of this.

H: Yeah, and we can have a running play and let Connie score.

W: Of course!

H: And then spike the ball!

W: Of course. She can do her little victory dance. We'll have to coach her, I mean, show her all the moves we want her to make. Of course if you tell her to throw the ball down and dance around when she scores, she'll really enjoy that.

Comment: The therapy team listened to the preceding family conversation and allowed it to continue due to the way it enacted a resourceful context. The couple discussed the task with enthusiasm and humour. At this point the therapist reenters the room and begins moving the session to closure.

TH: Okay, I'm just going to go over it one more time, you know, because I think this is so important for your father. One thing that one of the team members thought of is, given the kind of relationship that you have with your Mom, she may say that she doesn't want to do it.

W: She may not say it but it'll be, "Well, I don't know. I'm tired. . . ." It'll be all these excuses.

TH: Well if she does not want to play, she can come and be a fan.

W: If I could get her to the location, I think she would be the coach—that's what she would do. Because she always gets Daddy—the last few years they've had trouble, she has been trying to tell him how to coach after he loses the ball game. I think her being coach would be perfect. We may have to work around to it, but I think we can probably work something out.

TH: We really want you to give some thought to what kind of plays you're going to run. And for me, it would be kind of nice to see your daughter have the winning touchdown run.

W: We've already discussed that. We are going to show her how to spike the ball, and how to do the end-zone dance.

TH: Wow! You guys are way ahead of me . . .

W: See, this is right up my alley, because when you've grown up around coaching and football all your life, you know . . .

TH: Okay. How long do you think it'll take you to get it all together and get the film?

W: First I'm going to call Mother tonight and line up a day for her to come to town. Then I'll call my friend and see if she will videotape it for us, and we'll just go from there and try to get it done as soon as possible.

TH: And you know that going out to buy the ball should involve just the three of you, your daughter and you two, separate from Mom.

W: Uh-huh, oh yea, right.

TH: Okay, so after you've played the game, made the videotape, and all four of you have signed the ball, we'd like the four of you to get together and look at the film, to make sure that you're happy with how it turned out . . .

W: Okay.

TH: Then, if you're happy with it, set up a time where you can go and surprise your father with it.

W: It sounds like fun.

TH: You know, I think this is a very important thing. But, of course, you also know this has to do with much more than just your Dad.

W: Oh yeah—it's the whole family.

TH: Yea.

Comment: The team telephone with some suggestions.

TH: One final word from the team—we would like you to come back here in a month for another talk. That is when the team will be back. I may want to see you one time between then and now, but there's one final word from the team: when you two and Connie go out shopping for the ball, it is important that Connie be the one who selects the ball.

W: Okay.

TH: And you can tell her you are doing this for grandpa. Okay?

W: She'll get a big kick out of that.

TH: And you might want to think about whether you want to bring Connie and even your mother back for the next session.

That will be up to you, or just the two of you come, whatever you want.

W: Okay, great. That really sounds like lots of fun.

TH: Alright. You take care.

* * *

The next chapter presents another case in which football is involved. In this case the identified client is a former professional football player. The connection between these two cases will become apparent as the cases unfold.

CHAPTER FOUR

The spell

ACT I: THE SET-UP

J ames, a former professional football player for seven years with a champion team in the US National Football League, and his second wife, Mary, a well-educated professional, came for therapy. James had been in and out of psychiatric institutions around two to four times a year for the past nine years. Diagnosed as "schizophrenic", he stays at home and receives complaints from his wife that he doesn't do anything.

When James and Mary got married, his first wife, Sandy, told him, "Your marriage is not going to last a month". In their divorce settlement James lost everything except the bedroom furniture, which is presently used in his second marriage. Within three months after his first wife, Sandy, making this proclamation, he was in a psychiatric institution for the first of many times.

With these presenting lines and themes focusing on James as "sick" and "crazy", the therapist moved toward Act II, where the new theme is introduced of the couple having a "spell" cast on them by his first wife. In this theme, both James and Mary can work

37

together to break the spell, which is a more resourceful theme than dealing with James as sick and crazy.

Throughout this case the following abbreviations will be used:

TH = Therapist,   CN = Consultant
J   = James, husband   M   = Mary, wife

ACT II: CREATING THE RESOURCEFUL CONTEXT

TH: Brad and I have been talking about your situation for about the last hour. And I've been filling him in on what we've done over the last year, your past hospitalizations, and all. And we are real fortunate that Brad is here, because, in addition to being a well-known family therapist he has conducted research on traditional healing practices used around the world. He just got back from Africa, as a matter of fact. He's been over there studying tribal healing and this may become useful.

J: Sure. Sure.

TH: Uh, this is what Brad's ideas were when I described for him everything you and I have talked about. Um ... last night, Mary, you said that it's time ... that you're tired of putting things off with Sandy, and it's time to put her behind you. And James, you agreed with what she said. You said you were ready for that. Well, I couldn't agree more. But you see, I think, and Brad agrees, that we've been on the right track on a lot of things that we've talked about over the last year, involving Sandy and involving, I don't know if you want ... I'm sure you remember, what we were talking about is that it's almost as though Sandy were trying to put a spell on you. She had said that "You won't last a month. You will not have a month of happiness." That really struck me as significant, and in a lot of ways, she's succeeded.

Comment: The transformational hinge that attempts to move the case from addressing the impoverished theme of a "psychotic man" to a more resourceful theme involves specifying the former wife's "spell".

J: I don't know if she succeeded. She said if we got married we wouldn't stay together a month.

TH: But listen, that's what hit us, back there, like a lightning bolt. When Sandy said . . . Here, first of all, I was wrong thinking that Sandy's spell was not a strong one. In effect, it has been a powerful, powerful spell, and right now, it's time to break it. I couldn't agree more with you on it. You walked in here and you said, "It's time to put her behind us." And you were right on target. You [James] agreed. But listen, here it is, you were saying how in the world it could be nine years since the two of you married. Well, it hasn't been nine years, James. I don't want to mess with your time, or anything like that, but it's as though . . . she said it won't last a month, and when she said that, in effect, when she said that, you were frozen in time. That's the bottom line. As a couple, you're frozen in time. You are frozen in time. It's like it's four days after she said that. It's like it's only been four days since Sandy made this statement to you that it's not going to last a month, and you guys have been frozen in time. It is as though nothing has changed. You have been doing the same thing over and over again. One example that happened just now was when you, Mary, said, "I don't tell you what to do all the time". And I'm sure that's the truth. I'm sure you don't. But, in effect, what she did by saying that you won't last a month was that she got going this kind of misunderstanding between the two of you. You haven't lived nine years of happiness, you've lived nine years of being at odds with each other. (James nodded his head in agreement.) Not every minute, sometimes, occasionally, you have a 30-minute reprieve—that is in a week or something. Ten minutes here and there. But you're stuck. Stuck still asking the question, "Is she right? Is it going to last a month?" And let me tell you something right now, what I don't think you have clear in your head, I know you've heard it and said it, you're not going to like this word, but this whole last ten years has been spent proving that you're not going to last a month.

Comment: The therapist defines the spell as the couple being frozen in time and reframes the past nine years as four days. This enables all previous descriptions of unexplained conduct to be accounted for by a temporal "pathology". The whole nine years of complaints are reduced to one question regarding when the spell will be broken. Note that the spell, as temporally defined, will be logically broken when the couple realizes that they really have stayed together for more than one month.

TH: I know this may sound crazy, but this is a crazy situation.

J: It doesn't sound crazy.

TH: You know, it's like, you may be at day 29, maybe. Or maybe 24, I don't know.

ACT III: PRESCRIPTION FOR ENACTING THE RESOURCEFUL CONTEXT

CN: I want to let you know how convinced we are, to add a voice to the chorus.

J: Okay.

CN: The spell is strong. She said you won't last more than a month. Do you know how easy it is to break the spell? All you had to say is, "We went past a month". The spell would be broken. She froze you into thinking you haven't gone past a month. But it has been nine years. All you've got to do is say, "We've gone nine years and the spell is broken". When you get that in your head, the furniture is going to be gone.

Comment: The temporal definition of the spell is restated and re-emphasized. In addition a means of breaking it is set forth as the couple coming to grips with the recognition that they have been together nine years. Furthermore, it is suggested that when the spell is broken they will know that the bedroom furniture must be moved.

J: Didn't I tell you that right away?

M: I just found that out when we started coming here.

CN: But you see how his life's been? Typically, when you first break up, it takes a while to get back on your feet. To get back in the world, and so forth. But if you're frozen in time, what's going to happen? You'll have nine years to look like you're in a one-month thing.

J: I understand.

CN: That's powerful stuff, so I think it's time to talk to the man about moving forward with getting that furniture out. They can't do it all at one time—just a piece at a time.

J: Hold it, Brad, let me say this about that. (Turning to Mary) What did I tell you the other day, that wasn't the first time I told you about us being frozen.

TH: Feeling like you're frozen?

J: What did I say the other day about the routine we're in. Not that I'm against it, not that I don't love being at home, being a homebody. You know what I said about that? That was recently.

M: You're always saying something about we don't do anything, it's just the same old thing.

CN: I would guess for you, that if you'd get inside your head, that probably what irritates you more than anything is wanting somehow to say to him and to you and to both of you, "Let's get on with it!"

TH: Get on with it!

CN: Let's go ahead. Let's move on. Does that make any sense to you? Do you have a frustration at things being stuck?

Comment: The therapy team will reframe all lines offered by clients as understandable in light of their frozen temporal state.

J: I sure do.

CN: And then you need to realize how much work. It is harder work to sit and be frozen. It feels frozen.

Comment: James's inactivity, previously negatively connoted, is now understood as hard work when viewed in the context of a frozen temporal spell.

J: I tell her it's the hardest job in the world.

CN: It's unbelievable. It's a spell and the thing about it is, it's as simple as realizing that it has been nine years.

M: You've got to do it.

CN: It's been nine years . . .

J: And I'm not saying to her to help me, you know, get out of this or saying that she should do something, but in a way, I am. In a way, I'm saying to her, "Hey, why don't we do . . . ?" She used to say, "Look, why don't you go?"

TH: But you see what happens? I think, because you used the word in there—"decoys". If you're a hunter, it's a decoy. You two get into a spat over this or that, or you name it, they're decoys. They take you off the scent.

CN: And that's not the issue. Sandy is irritating you, getting him to do this, or getting him to do what he thinks is a good idea. All that stuff is just natural relationship crap. I mean, who was it that said, "marriage is hell. The only thing worse is being single"? You know? I mean, this is part of the stuff that goes with being married. On the other hand, there are frustrations, but they're side effects of this other thing. Don't get confused with it. The thing at hand here is to realize that you've survived nine years.

TH: Next month it's ten. Their anniversary is in a month from now.

CN: Ten years. It's been ten years. Get this into your head and the spell will be broken, you can get on with your life and you can get that damn furniture out of . . .

J: It's time to do it now.

Comment: The therapy team directly suggests that they wake up from the spell. The couple will be given specific instructions to take action immediately. As will be seen, the team will encourage them to leave the session, go to their home, and perform a task the enactment of which is verification that the spell has been broken.

TH: That's the power of the spell. It's time to do it now. You said it yesterday.

CN: (Leaving) I'm going to let you talk.

TH: ... It's time to do it now. Maybe you are thinking it's premature, this furniture business, but I tell you what, I don't think you need to think about it, I think maybe it's time to do something.

J: It is time to start.

TH: If you can't do it all at once, take one piece at a time. Take a knob off of one of the dressers, you know, to start. But start. And get it done. Stop acting like you're only going to last a month. Realize that you've lasted ten years. You've got an anniversary coming up. What better anniversary gift than to put some ashes from the burnt-up bedroom furniture on her lawn.

J: I understand. I understand. (Nodding in affirmation)

TH: If you only carve off one little piece a night, then do it. It's time to do something. It's time to clean house. As much as I love talking to you two, it's costing you a ton of money to come here, you know? And I'm cheap compared to other things. It's time to do something. Tonight, Mary, if you were to take one piece, one part off the furniture, tonight, what would it be? What would you do? As a starting point, take one little piece off of that furniture, as a way to start. What would it be?

Comment: The therapy team will not back up from pushing the couple to wake up from the spell. This constant challenge is done to keep the conversation focused on the resourceful theme. From the perspective of RFT, the therapy team is not pushing to change the clients, but attempting to stabilize the resourceful context that is emerging of a couple addressing how to face a frozen marital spell jointly.

M: One little piece off?

TH: Yes, as a way of saying, we're going to start tonight, and then go from there. It's time to start.

J: Basically, you have two night tables, two lamps, bed and frame, a chest of drawers, and a dresser. Now, the appearance of it, it's a nice-looking thing but the idea of ... but it is beyond that. I wasn't thinking clearly. That bedroom set should have been the last thing I kept.

TH: I don't think it's coincidental that she left that particular thing with you. I'm sorry. Whether she meant to do it, conscious, unconscious, the fact is she left you the bed and said your marriage to Mary will not last a month.

Comment: The consultant enters the room.

CN: I just want to point out the power of the spell.

TH: Yeah.

CN: You can't even come up with a piece. What I would like to do is to let them have a discussion. If you tonight got rid of something . . . if you find that you have to go small, it may be just a piece of the lamp-shade. Is it fabric? Something you can cut?

Comment: The couple's hesitation to agree over what they can get rid of is cited as further evidence of the spell. Thus, their reluctance to take action is utilized as further verification that action is necessary. In this way all client lines are woven into substantiating and elaborating the resourceful context.

J: Yeah.

CN: It may be something small. The spell may be so much that the first thing you do is just take a little piece and get it out. I mean, this may be too overwhelming to think of a whole lamp, or a whole chunk of furniture.

J: I have to give Mary credit for this. As far as changes, she's rigid, rigid, as a 90-year old . . .

TH: Look at your wife's face.

M: Talk about changes—him. Have I ever wanted it out? It never came across my mind. The only thing that concerned me when he . . . we didn't have to buy bedroom furniture because he had that from his settlement. But I did not want the mattress.

TH: See, you had a sense of it.

CN: See, that's the power of the spell. It's never come across your mind. It's never come across your mind that you've gone past a month. I mean, it's not ... my sense is, and I just want to invite you to talk about what piece could you comfortably get rid of tonight. Because, I think you'd be amazed if you ended up sleeping on the floor, and nothing in that room, as opposed to what you're in now. Just the power, this is what has held your life. .... If you had to get rid of something, that you could actually do it. It may be such a tiny thing, just a clip out of the shade.

J: Well, I want Mary ... now you talked to us about this and you got us both to agree, and I asked Mary what about it, and she wasn't really ... but here we go again.

M: She wasn't?

CN: Is this her house you live in? Is it her bedroom?

TH: See, I asked that. I asked that.

CN: You may need to go into another room, and lock the door, until you're ready to get that out of there.

TH: I asked them that last night. I said, "How many bedrooms do you have? You have Joey, you've got yourselves, and what was your daughter's. And now it's used as a whatever room. It might be ... see, here's what I think, James, I don't think Mary is rigid in particular. In fact, I think you're going to be tickled by the effects of breaking the spell.

CN: Let's find out. Let's give them five minutes to see if they can agree upon some one little thing that they could take out of that room.

TH: See, I think you're going to be tickled pink to get out of this rut, but, what I think it is, is that we all have ... me, I'm number one, I'm supposed to be the damn expert here, I underestimated this spell, big time. That's this ... this spell is not just freezing you, James, it's freezing you too Mary. Now five minutes, I'm going to get out of here and let you talk.

CN: We'll see what happens.

TH: Not only does it freeze you, but it freezes you into accusing each other of being the slow-poke.

CN: I don't think that in five minutes they can agree on anything in that room.

J: Hey, that's a tall statement.

Comment: Having challenged the couple, the therapist and consultant leave the room to observe the couple's interaction.

J: Listen, Mary, when he says it lasted a month, that's the first time it came up, when he asked whether we were still sleeping . . . when he asked us point blank whether we were still sleeping in the same bed or something like that.

M: That bed wasn't the furniture, James. It's the bedroom set.

J: But you understand what they're saying about . . .

M: Yes, now we're supposed to be making a decision if we were going to get rid . . .

J: I wrote those people who were having sales that weekend and this lady, but I didn't say anything to you about it. All I was concerned about at that point was just getting rid of the headboard, but uh . . . we can go for the whole thing. I think it would be refreshing. I think that would be positive.

M: And you're ready to burn it up?

J: I'm ready to get it out of there.

M: Burn it up!

J: Now, I'm not saying I'm cheap or anything, but the appearance of the bedroom suite is . . . that maybe what has us kind of . . . it appears to be a nice outfit, but it's more than that. What's behind it should be over.

M: What piece do you want to get rid of? Tonight, which piece?

J: Let's get a lamp-shade out of there, at least. Otherwise, when . . . what we're going to have to do is just go put a bedroom suite on layaway and that way it's set up, we're going to have to get rid of everything, because there is stuff in everything. So we're going to have to do it all, pretty much.

M: And we're going to chop it up for firewood?

J: We're going to have to get it out of there. (They both laugh)

I don't think it'll be a spell enough to . . . to keep from fretting about we gave it to such and such a couple and they had bad luck. . . . we gave them a piece of this and a piece to them and they had bad luck . . .

Comment: The therapy team is satisfied with the couple's maintained presence in the resourceful context. At this point the therapist reenters the room.

TH: Five minutes just flies by. Listen now, I think this is so important. Number 1—I'll tell you what, as I was walking out the door, I think you're frozen in time, both of you, not just you, James, and I think you're frozen into bickering at each other about mundane junk, that keeps you stuck. Okay, and if it's not mundane stuff, then you're frozen in . . . in accusing the other of being stuck. You know? You tell each other. We just overheard you say, "Maybe a lamp-shade, a lamp-shade tonight". Right? What we want to know is by when can you do this? Because we want to give you a call to make sure.

J: Now that would be more than a small piece, that would be major, more or less, being an uncovered lamp.

M: You're the one that suggested a lamp-shade.

J: We've got to start somewhere. We've got junk in everything. So we have to make plans to just go the same route. And then change over, and get everything changed out.

TH: Just relatively nice furniture is expensive. I mean, it's not easy to replace a bedroom set. In this day and time it's expensive. I personally think that a good thing for you to do is to shut the damn door on that room, use your spare bedroom, and take the furniture out as you can.

J: Well, there's one right across the hall from the other one.

TH: My point is to just take action. If you can't take a whole lamp shade, take your scissors, take a knife, cut a piece of lamp shade out, do whatever you've got to do to start.

M: Oh, we can cut a piece of the lamp shade out.

TH: Let's not let this be the only thing you do in the next two weeks.

J: I want Mary to be in agreement totally about this. I under-
      stand, you know, wholeheartedly what you're saying about
      that. It's a symbol and I said to her that the appearance of the
      bedroom suite—it's nice-looking, carved . . .

M: It's not that nice.

CN: Man, this is a tough spell! I heard you in there saying, "let's get
      it all out". And then when I said, "Let's get the lamp-shade
      out", you said, "Well . . ."

J: I take the blame. I had to be a damn fool for bringing it in the
      house in the first place.

TH: You can't be blamed for doing that. It's the spell, you're not to
      blame.

CN: It's the spell, you have no responsibility. You agree to go
      straight home, take something out and burn it?

TH: And don't do too much. What is important is that you start
      small.

Comment: The therapy team repeatedly reframes the couple's
blaming as a consequence of the spell. With this understanding, the
couple's disagreements do not necessarily lead to distancing them,
but may paradoxically join them by renewing their desire to break
the spell.

TH: One little thing?

CN: Can you agree to one?

M: We can cut a piece out of that lamp.

TH: And you're going to cut it up? A little at a time.

J: Yeah.

CN: The last thing that I want to say to you is think about this: the
      longer that furniture stays in there, the more therapy you
      people are going to need to get and you start adding that up,
      and you've got furniture. Do you hear what I'm saying?

TH: You could have paid for that furniture 40 times.

M: Is this some of kind of African Ritual? That's in the back of my
      mind. (Laughing)

CN: No, no, no.

TH: We talked about this months ago.

M: Yeah, I know we talked about it, but I know James too.

TH: You know what I think about you and Mary right now? I think this is the part of the spell where you accuse him of being a slow-poke and he accuses you and if it's not that way around he's accusing you of being a slow-poke and what happens is you stay right where you're at, and nothing changes.

J: I think you're right.

CN: I think they should argue all they want, but I think what they should do tonight is agree on a time and you call them and say that something is out of that room and burned. That's it. Even if it's just a tiny little piece.

J: When?

TH: When you're ready.

CN: So I'll be seeing you.

J: When?

TH: He's saying in a month probably, because he's going to be back in a month.

J: You'll be back in a month?

CN: I will and good luck to you because . . .

J: Okay, we should be clear . . .

TH: You should be clear by the time I call you tonight.

J: Oh yeah, yes. (Turning to Mary) You are going to be seeing to that.

M: I thought we were supposed to do it together—we.

TH: We are going to decide on something.

CN: The only thing that I worry about with you is not pissing people off, it's just finding ways to piss people off that you can enjoy. There's a little thing about it. When you get to the top in playing football, that pisses a lot of people off.

TH: Oh, it pisses a lot of people off. You know who it pissed off, Brad? It pissed off his brothers. I'll bet you.

M: They played football too.

TH: Don't tell me they weren't competing over who was the best.

J: One of them said that I was the best athlete. That was a little more sarcastic than whatever, just really, I would just like to . . .

CN: One thing I want to say about you because I have to run is that if you . . . you said . . . you've got a crazy part too. See, I think you are both crazy.

M: I have to be.

CN: But the whole trick is how to enjoy your craziness.

M: I enjoy it.

CN: Well, just get this spell out of your life.

J: I say that she used to have a sense of humour and then I thought I had one, you know, but uh . . .

TH: And Sandy just sucked it right out of your marriage. I bet nine years ago you guys were something to be around.

CN: I'll tell you something else, when you guys get it out of that room tonight and burn it, it's got to be burned. You're going to find that your sense of humour is going to tempt you to not take it seriously and get the giggles. I think this should be done seriously.

J: I agree.

CN: You should do that as seriously as you can be. Because it's going to seem silly looking at him dragging out a huge hunk of that furniture . . . and you take it seriously because this is really serious.

TH: Serious, and it's only the first step.

Comment: The therapists connote the task as "serious" and warn them about laughing. This is paradoxically intended to escalate the absurdity of the task with the hope that the couple will be unable to resist the temptations of healing laughter.

CN: Absolutely.

TH: When can I call you tonight to see how it goes?

J: After 9:00.

TH: OK, between 9:00 and 9:30 I'll give you a call.

J: Okay.

TH: The lamp-shade looks like it's winning the race, but it doesn't matter to me what piece it is. Part of a piece. And like Brad said, maybe we're starting too big. Maybe we have to start small. I hear your point. You can't just throw your clothes in a pile in a corner of the bedroom.

J: Well, we could, you know. That would provoke bringing in a new set of furniture.

TH: You [James] can be in charge of getting it out of the room, and you [Mary] can be in charge of burning it. Then you [James] can both chop it up together if you need to, because you're a pretty strong guy and wielding an ax maybe is hard work. Look at me. I ain't done it in a long time but I remember what it's all about. But uh . . . you be in charge of getting it out of the room, and you be in charge of burning it up and keep those ashes because you've got something else you have to do with those. Okay? Alright. You got a job ahead of you. Let me say one more thing. If you begin to find yourself not doing anything with this, would you just remind yourself that you keep underestimating how damn strong this spell is. Because Sandy is as present in your life right now as she was nine years ago when she said that you won't last a month.

J: I agree with you there. I . . . you know, I'm not blaming Mary with anything . . .

TH: You're both under the spell.

J: Yeah, both of us.

TH: You're both under a spell, and that woman . . .

J: It has to be done together . . .

TH: You can't do it alone. Neither of you can do it on your own.

J: I can't get her to do anything . . .

TH: You can't do it on your own, you don't want to do it alone. The effect of that spell is so strong that it might provoke you into accusing the other of dragging their feet, you know, and then the next thing you know you're going around in circles and you get caught up in the bullshit that has nothing to do with the spell which I think is at the centre of it. I can't wait to call you at 9:30 to find out what you decided to burn.

J: I can tell you there will be a hole right in the front, so every time you go in the room you'll see the bulb . . . It will jump out at us.

TH: Yeah, you'll see it. And then the next time something else—maybe a hole on the other side.

Comment: Later that night we called James and Mary. They had cut out a hole in the lampshade and were unable to stop giggling on the phone. We reminded them of the seriousness of the situation and congratulated them on the action they had taken.

CHAPTER FIVE

The family football game

S everal weeks after the previously described session with James and Mary, we decided to call James and ask him to serve as a consultant on the case with the police couple who had been instructed to play and film a family football game. They had been unable to complete the assignment, so we hired James to be a football consultant to help them carry out the task.

In this consultation session, Hal and Wanda brought their daughter, Connie, and were introduced to our consultant, James.

The following abbreviations will be used to designate participants in this session:

TH	= Therapist,	CN	=	Consultant
W	= Wanda, wife	H	=	Hal, husband
C	= Connie, daughter	TH	=	Therapist

ACT I: INTRODUCING THE COACH

TH: (to Connie, the daughter) Hi, I'm Wendel. It's nice to meet you. Oh gosh, she's got me and she won't let go. How are you all?

H: Fine.

TH: It's good to see you.

W: It's good to be back.

TH: I want you to know that we have a rare opportunity. We were thinking about what you told me on the phone about how it was difficult to get your mother involved in getting this assignment done.

W: Uh-huh.

TH: Actually, that has turned out to our advantage in many respects.

W: Oh? Okay.

TH: We have the privilege of having a former professional football player as part of our team today . . .

Comment: James, whose previous experiences of being in therapy contexts over the last nine years marked him as "psychotic", is now preparing to enter a therapy session where he is introduced as a resourceful expert and consultant.

W: Wow!

TH: Yeah, he came in at a special request to do a consultation with us in working with you all, as a matter of fact.

W: Neat!

TH: He played for eight years in the national football league, he played six years for Atlanta Falcons, and two years with . . .

H: What! What's his name?

TH: James Jackson.

H: Oh yeah! Yeah. See, I'm an Atlanta fan.

TH: No kidding. We'll get James to autograph the ball for you.

H: Great!

W: Neat, neat.

TH: What we were thinking was, since you're having some trouble getting your mother involved, and since Christmas is right around the corner, uh . . . we asked James to come in to help you a little bit . . . do you have any plays that you put together?

W: I was waiting to kind of get it lined out . . .

H: We were . . . no, go ahead . . .

W: No, I wasn't going to try to, you know, get Connie involved too far ahead of time, because then, we might have the beans spilled. I was just trying to hang loose until we kind of got something set, and of course, nothing got set, and so . . . we never really went that far.

TH: We were thinking what a nice gift for your Dad for Christmas . . . is this video.

W: Yeah.

H: Yeah.

TH: And so, I guess, the best thing for us to do is to go ahead and ask James to come in so he can talk with you a little bit. He brought his son Joey, so that'll be kind of cool.

W: Well . . . I wish I'd changed clothes now.

TH: James Jackson, I want you to meet Hal, Wanda, and Connie.

W: Nice to meet you.

J: I have Joey over here. What's your last name?

H: Landley.

J: Yeah? So you've heard of me?

H: Oh yeah.

J: I played from '73 to '81.

H: Uh-huh. You played when they had John Smith and uh . . . let me think who all was there. Bill Bryant . . .

J: Yeah.

H: All those old-timers.

J: Rob Hall . . .

H: Ned Jones . . .

J: Jones . . .

H: Uh, who was the center?

J: Uh . . . Jessie Robert first, and then Al Kramer took over . . . Sanders from Georgia, I think . . . he was another center that played during that . . . just before I left.

W: Where did you play college ball?

J: Arkansas.

W: Oh, okay. No wonder you're around here then.

J: So you work with law enforcement.

W: Both of us do. I just got off from work.

J: What's your last name?

H: Landley

J: Oh, okay.

C: My last name is Newly.

W: That's right.

J: Your last name is Newly?

W: Yeah, she's from my first marriage, so she has a different last name.

J: Hey, this is my second one here. I had three children by my first wife, and a son now who is probably a year older than her. He wears glasses too.

W: Really?

J: So, it ain't easy.

W: Does he go through them as fast as this one does?

J: No.

W: Oh really? Boy, she can go through them in a hurry. Hers are so stretched right now it's terrible.

J: He uh, takes pretty good care of his glasses. He has this strap that makes him able to take care of them.

W: Yeah, maybe so. Yeah. She leaves them laying around too much.

H: The dog got a hold of them.

W: Yeah, the dog chewed on one of her ear pieces and all that.

ACT II: SETTING UP THE GAME

TH: What I was thinking you could do is tell them a story about maybe teamwork, and then if we can get them to develop a play, could you go back behind the mirror with me, and we'll watch them on camera as they put together some plays. And if they run into a jam, you could come back in and help them get the play straight, and then they will go out and do it. What do you think, Coach?

J: Nothing really comes to mind, because I'm not much of a story-teller ... but they know, alright, first-hand about team work in the type of jobs you have ...

H: Uh-huh.

TH: ... I don't care what you do, it involves teamwork. Everybody can't be the head coach, even in a family. I thought I was the head coach for years, and I probably wasn't. But everybody can be a member of the team. Everybody's got to be a member of the team. And you need that feedback from everybody, from center to the others, to ... somebody has to take the initiative, or the responsibility, of being in charge, you know, but that may not be 50/50 in some families. It may be some-thing ...

H: And in some it's going to be a little bit more than others ...

J: A little more ... yeah.

W: That's true. It makes a lot of sense.

J: You have to accept that, and you have to know who that person is, and ... you just can't ... everyone has to be sup-portive. You said they [the therapy team] had something in mind ...

TH: No, no ... What I was thinking was that they might work on putting a play together, maybe ... and we can watch them on the camera while they work at it, as a family, and then if they get stuck, you can come back in and help them out.

J: I'll tell you ... You can do that ... But what I had in mind is ... if you play flag football, I brought this little flag, and since it's just three of you ... and you just got off work.

W: Yeah, and this time I said, "Ah, I don't need to change clothes like I did last time". So, yeah ... I wish I had changed clothes now. I'll be the quarterback. You don't have to run so much.

TH: We could get Joey to work out.

J: I brought him, yeah . . . Uh . . . uh . . . that's not a good idea either. I'll tell you, maybe a couple of warm-up calisthenics. And uh . . .

W: Like do a pre-game warm-up and all that? That sounds good.

J: Not enough to tire anybody out.

W: Please, no. I'm anaemic right now anyway.

J: Just a little stretching and then we'll play football. You know, we'll set that up. Unless you had something that you wanted to do.

H: No, no. We hadn't . . . I'm listening.

W: No, not really. I had just run some little thoughts through my mind . . . but nothing major.

TH: That was Brad on the phone. He said that he would like for us to go out and play some flag football, but before we go, let's let them take a couple of minutes and see if they can come up with one or two simple plays . . . by themselves, and then as soon as they've got that . . . you can take them out, lead them through the calisthenics, and have a little game. Alright?

J: Alright.

Comment: The therapists and the coach [James] leave the room to observe as Hal, Wanda, and Connie work together.

W: Sounds good. Okay, we have to decide who's going to play what position.

H: Alright. I suggest this . . .

W: Okay, what?

H: I'm going to always be the quarterback.

W: You?

H: I'm kidding. I'll let you be the quarterback.

W: Okay.

H: I'll be the center, and she can be the running back/receiver.

W: Did you hear that? You're going to be the running back/receiver.

H: You're going to be the one that catches the ball.

W: Do you know what that means?

C: Okay. Yeah, I'll catch it.

Comment: The family spent about 10 minutes coming up with some plays, including a running and a passing play. They drew diagrams of the plays and discussed them so that everyone understood their role. James then reentered the room and told them how impressed he was with their knowledge of the game. He then led them outside to play a game.

ACT III: THE FOOTBALL GAME

James, the family, and the entire therapy team walked to a field next to the clinic. Two pairs of therapists joined arms to create goal posts at each end of the playing field. One therapist was the game official and another carried a portable video camera. Other team members stood along the side-lines and cheered for the team.

James led the family through a series of warm-up exercises, and the game official then declared that the game was to begin. As the following transcript indicates, James told the family team to begin with the passing play they had designed.

J: Okay, Connie they're going to throw the ball. Your Daddy's going to throw the ball. Alright. Come back, and . . .

C: Okay. (giggling)

W: When I say, "GO", you take off . . .

C: Okay.

H: Can you go up there with the . . .

J: Alright.

W: Set. Hup one, hup two, hup three . . .

Comment: At this moment the family initiated its first play. The mother threw an incomplete pass to the daughter and the family decided to try the same play again.

J: Uh, yeah. Connie, don't go as far this time Connie . . .

W: Just go right . . . right over . . . come over this way. . . . Okay?
      Ready? Go. Shift, set, hup one, hup two, hup three, woah,
      woah, turn around and stop . . . watch it . . . alright!!!!

Comment: Connie almost catches the ball and the crowd cheers.
Mother shouts, "Yeah, way to win a game! Yeah Sarah!" Play continues:

W: This time, you just take off that way . . . we've got four plays
      for you to catch the ball, and when I tell you I'm going to turn
      and I'm going to hand you the ball, then you start running that
      way, and Daddy's going to take off and run that way with you
      to keep all the defensive players off of you.

C: Okay.

W: And then you're going to run down there to that goal line, and
      score. You see the goal posts down there. Goal posts—come to
      attention.

Comment: The family is directing the therapists in how to participate
in a resourceful way in the game.

W: (To daughter) I'm just going to give it to you and you're going
      to run towards them because they're our goal posts. This time,
      I'm just going to say, the first time I say, "Hup", that's when
      I'm going to turn and give it to you. Okay? Set, hup . . .

Comment: Connie grabbed the ball and ran as hard as she could
toward the goal posts with the crowd yelling "Go, Go, Go. Run
Connie!" When she scored the touchdown, everyone applauded.

W: Way to go! Is this a real football game, or what? Way to go.
      Okay. We won!

H: We won! We won! Do you want to do it again?

W: That was it! That was serious!

C: Hey, it's Daddy first. Mamma, Mamma . . .

H: Mamma's not going to . . . she was the center on that one.

D: Mamma, it's your turn now.

W: Oh, it's my turn to be the runner now, nah . . . we'll do that one later. We'll do that one at home.

H: Are we going to run any more plays? You have a play for us? Do you want to give us a special play? Or are you satisfied with what we're doing.

J: I am completely satisfied with this team.

W: I agree, it turned great!

C: Can I give Daddy a squeeze hug?

H: Yeah, come on.

Comment: The consultant suggested to the coach and family that since this was being filmed as a Christmas present, it would be great to have an old-fashioned movie ending. James was asked to tell the team what his coach used to tell the Atlanta Falcons after they won a big game. James had everyone, family and therapists, join hands and he then shouted out, "Good luck, gang, let's win this thing in 90's!" Everyone shouted a victory cry. James turned to Connie, handed her the game ball, saying "this is for you". She then asked him to sign it. Following his signing, she jumped into his arms with a big hug. James threw his towel over his shoulder and with his son Joey by his side walked off into the sunset, all recorded in grand Hollywood style.

AFTER THE GAME:
FOLLOW-UP WITH WANDA AND HAL

A follow-up session with Wanda and Hal was conducted several weeks after the football game. The therapeutic effort was to maintain the resourceful contexts constructed in previous sessions.

ACT I: THE SET-UP

In the beginning of the session, the therapist comments on all the professionals who have been involved in helping this family. Each professional has had an opinion, sometimes conflicting with the

others. Following this brief discussion, the therapist shifts to introducing the taped Family Football Game as a major resource for the
family. With this resource the therapist can suggest that the resourceful family on the videotape is not the same family described
by other professionals as problematic, hopeless, non-resourceful.

TH: Uh . . . glad to see you back.

W: I'm glad to be back. I don't know about him, but I know I am.

TH: And un . . . what we seem to have here is a mystery . . . you've
      seen a lot of professionals in the last . . . I don't know how long
      for sure it's been . . . at least two people at the Mental Health
      Center, and at least one psychiatrist. Uh, the therapist that
      referred you here. And me. That's at least five that I'm aware
      of. There may be more. You have a private doctor who's giv-
      ing you medication for your depression. Six. You've got your
      mother involved—seven. Your grandmother—who's a profes-
      sional or was, retired—eight. All of the opinions, and probably
      all of the varying opinions and this is part of the mystery that
      we find ourselves caught in here, because, you see, one of the
      funny things that we have, is we have a tape I want to show
      you, of a family that is a lot like you. Their daughter, the same
      age as yours, this couple are active. They are able to enjoy
      themselves with their kid. You can tell that this child is a
      normal kid, a lot of energy, but not out of control, necessarily.
      You know, the mom and dad, they're like all moms and dads,
      they differ on some things, but they're basically together on
      the essentials. And uh, the funny thing is that they look just
      like you. But they don't sound anything like what you've just
      described. Gosh, I think I've got the right tape here. Oh, I
      know where this came from. Because the family on this tape
      was not the family you just described.

W: Gosh, I hate watching and listening to myself . . .

ACT II: CREATING THE RESOURCEFUL CONTEXT

Comment: The videotape of the football game was played and the
therapist and family commented on what they saw.

H: You can see the happiness too. I need to be doing a lot of that.

TH: See, this is a family that looks good to me. Watch Connie now.

TH: (later) . . . You might want to write down his name—James Jackson.

W: My Daddy's already seen the football we all signed.

TH: Oh?

W: And Connie really enjoyed the game, without getting out of control. A lot of time, if we show her attention in any way, she will just lose it.

H: You can't do anything with her. I mean, it's like . . .

W: She stayed in control that time. That's what the difference is. She really did well that day.

W: She is a pretty good little player. She had a good time.

TH: This family here on the video is totally different from the one you just described to me.

Comment: The therapist excuses himself for discussion with the team and comes back with the following comments.

TH: I guess ten heads are better than one. They are thinking along the same line. They also see two different families. It is as though your family has a split personality. You've got the family that feels spooked. We don't know what spooks people. Don't know what sets it off. It could be any number of things. But the spooked family has a psychiatrist for their daughter, needs a therapist for you, has a grandmother who is really involved, to the point where it makes it too hard for you [Wanda] to do your job; the great-grandmother that is in there somewhere; the specialists at the Mental Health Center. They've got a lot of different things going on. But, in contrast to this, we have the family that plays together—the family that was on the film. The one that could make its own plays and carry them out. That can have a child that can play ball and not go too far. You know? It is such a striking difference between these two families. Uh . . . we really don't know what spooks you. It could be any number of things. But as I recall from our earlier conversations, one thing that spooks you is to have so many cooks in the kitchen.

Comment: The therapist is actually spelling out two choices of context that face the family—an impoverished context and a resourceful context. The former is called the "spooked family" and the latter is called the "family that plays together", the family that was on the film.

W: That and so many outside pressures, really, you know?

TH: Yes, all of it. And all of us, because I'm one too, all of us "experts" that are all alleged to know what they're doing, and they're just saying different things. I am not saying anything negative about anybody, but there are just so many different ways of looking at things. There is such a thing as having too many cooks in the kitchen, including grandma ... Uh, and grandpa for that matter. You know you worry about your Dad, that's a big one. Your background, from your family. I mean, all those things can be part of this spooked family. In contrast to a family that's a team. One of the very interesting things that James said about you after you left was, "I'm really struck with the fact that these people know how to play as a team." I'm not making that up, I can show you the tape, because I taped him saying that. I'm struck by that too. So it seems to me that our job is to help you get in touch with that, rather than the spooked model. Now I think at times in your past, you've been a team. The way you describe the first two years of your marriage, to me, sounds like a team. Uh, this three-week period you had less than a month ago, or something like that, you were working as a team. So, some of the things that could have spun you off, made you spook, were you worrying about your Dad's health, or him not doing so well, his coaching?—that makes you and your Mom nervous. That would be natural. Amongst many other things. Not even counting the stress of being a cop. I was a cop for five years. I know that stress. We're not going to even add that. But that's always there. Plus you guys have been talking about moving to Dallas, I'm not making that up am I?

W: No, it's in the background.

TH: See, these are all different things that can keep you from being a team. We know there is nothing wrong with the family that plays together. We think you guys have it together. You're an all-American family. I could show this film to anybody, as a demonstration of a normal family. But the spooked family needs medicine. That's all there is to it. They need medicine. And we've got some medicine that I want you to try for a month. Then I want you to come back so I can see you again. Here is the medicine. Anytime that you feel like you're at the end of your rope with each other or with your Connie, or with your well-intentioned mother, you are to get together with Connie, and go to the television and watch the tape of the family that was out there playing as a team. That will be your medicine.

Comment: The therapist is beginning to move towards Act III where a medicine can be prescribed.

W: To remind us?

TH: To remind you that you have this capacity. See, I don't think your child is at the point of no return. She's 8 years old. Goodness gracious. Probably there's some difficulties, but this situation is not unsalvageable. And let that be a medicine, when things are to the point where you're really wondering if you're going to make it. Come together as a team, and watch the team film. Now, we will want to give it to your Dad, but we think it's real important that you keep this copy. I'll make you another copy for your father. Okay? But we really think that you need the medicine as much as or more than your father. Right now.

W: Sounds good to me.

H: Sounds good to me too.

W: Simple too. It's not going to be a lot of extra work.

TH: Do you see the two different families? Because it's so striking. And when you work together well, man, you do it well. Which just tells us that you have the capacity. You have this ability.

But when you're spooked, you get a little afraid. You start questioning any little thing that happens, it gets blown all out of proportion.

W: It seems to . . . kind of.

TH: Yeah, it seems to grow when it gets going . . .

H: Now, I wonder sometimes, it's like I was telling you that I didn't experience depression, but I've told her in the past, it's been for three months, I've been in depression and didn't even recognize it until I started reading some things about depression. I've lost interest in a lot of things, and she's seen it, but I didn't notice it.

W: It has been a lot longer than three months though.

TH: That was part of your letter to him?

W: No, not really. This letter had things to do with just my feelings about things.

H: See, the things that got triggered from the letter, got triggered, because I had some things that I wanted to talk to her about a situation that came up . . .

Comment: The consultant entered the therapy room with a message.

CN: I just wanted to say that this is the spooked family here. You read that stuff and you get spooked.

Comment: From this point on, any impoverished description can be attributed to the impoverished context, that is, the spooked family.

H: Uh-huh.

CN: You talk to certain people and you get spooked. You think about certain things, you know, certain times in life, things that are irritating, and you think about them too much and magnify them, they spook you and that spooks the other person. Then everybody gets spooked and it's out of control. That's the spooked family.

TH: . . . and your daughter picks it all up.

CN: And then she gets spooked. Then there's this other family who is superbowl material. I mean you have a man [James], who my son looked up in the record books, who said, "Now this family is a team". And I think you gave him the best, and I think it's time for you to start taking your medicine.

ACT III: PRESCRIPTION FOR ENACTING THE RESOURCEFUL CONTEXT

TH: You have just described an example of what what we are talking about. I mean, I can give you books to read where if you read them, they would sure scare you—and be very convincing, about depression and whatever. Such an idea feeds on itself.

So, what we would like you to do is when things get a little frayed at the edges, either of you, with the child or the mom, or with each other, yourself, you know, the medicine is to watch the movie. Always in the past, since you've been having difficulties, things—numerous different things—will happen that will get you a little spooked or skittish, the more we talk, the more, the richer the variety of things that have happened, that could . . . any one of which could sink a family. You know? Whether you think about your relationship with your Mom, or your relationship with your Mom and Dad and your brother, and your Mom's relationship with her mother and her brother, alone—any one of those would be enough . . .

W: It is a fascinating combination!

TH: Oh God. And then your child comes along and is caught right smack in the middle of the same kind of thing, and then you [Hal] come out of your first marriage, out of the blue you are told by your wife that she doesn't want to be married to you anymore. And you get spooked—God knows—that would make you spooked. Your relationship with your Pop and your family, any part of that, the job—I'm not going to go into all of that, but both of you have high-stress jobs. If either one of you had that job, it would be enough, but you have all these things that can happen, that have happened, and what, in addition to being spooked, it has been that when you got spooked, you ended up going and talking to somebody to get help. It started in your family, initially, but then the professionals after that accidentally, not intentionally I'm sure, instead of helping you calm things, spooked you even more. In effect, you got more spooked. When you've three or four professionals trying to help, me included, who accidentally, in trying to help you, spook you more. . . . things can really begin to look . . .

H: It can get petty bleak.

TH: Beautifully said—pretty bleak. It can cloud your ability to see the fact that you can be a happy family. You can be a family that works together well, like it is on that film. That's why the medicine is very important this time, for the next month. When you get spooked, and things will happen . . . you know things happen—that's life. Things are going to occur that will really rattle your cage. And then having a very rambunctious child which we failed to mention. How can I forget Connie? Before going to a professional, the first thing you need to do is rally your team. That's what we want you to try. Get together and watch your film. That's your medicine. To remind you, and it's very important to keep reminding yourself, that you can be a team, in the midst of all this crazy life.

H: That is what I was about to ask you. If one of us gets spooked, so to say, do we say, "Hey, I'm spooked and everybody get together and watch the film?"

TH: You know what this sounds like? This sounds like a decision your team needs to make. Not me. Because I'm trying to let you guys be the professionals for yourself for a while. Let us professionals back away for a little bit. You guys use your own medicine. You know what to do. You can make these decisions. Okay? I really look forward to seeing you in a month or so.

CASE FOLLOW-UP

In the six-month period following this session several follow-up interviews were conducted with the family. The daughter, Connie, has improved in conduct both at home and in school, and her grades have continued to improve. Wanda continues to report a dramatic improvement in her relationship with her mother and father and received a promotion at work. Therapy was discontinued with the understanding the family can return for a check-up if they feel it necessary to do so. The football game video, a copy of which was given to Wanda's father as a gift, continues to be a resource for them.

CHAPTER SIX

A history with voodoo:
follow-up with James and Mary

During the session just described, the therapy team, with James's son observing, openly expressed how skilfully James had proceeded to connect therapeutically with the family, and they repeatedly commented among themselves about James's natural therapeutic abilities. As he continued working with the family, one observer commented, "If someone were watching a tape of this without knowing any background, they would think he was a superb therapist".

Following the football game there were many unanticipated positive accounts of James's conduct with his own family. He was perceived as having strength and leadership. Mary described their son Joey as expressing genuine admiration in ways he never had before. In this session with James and Mary, James was more vocal and carried himself with noticeably more dignity.

The therapist and the team were surprised by a revelation from James and Mary about the history of his first wife's (Sandy) involvement in the practice of voodoo. This included an account of their seeking spiritual help to break any "hex" Sandy or her family had put on them. What the therapist had not previously realized was that therapy had entered a resourceful context that was congruent with the family's previous history.

ACT I: THE SET-UP

TH: I was telling Brad about our last session, the last time we talked, and he was very interested in what you had been telling me about that time, a long time ago, when you were just having problems, and you had found out that Sandy was involved in witchcraft, or voodoo, or whatever. I don't remember. And you [Mary] went with his [James] mother and father to Houston to talk to somebody. He was very interested about that. Could you just give me a brief retelling of that story so he could hear it from you rather than my trying to remember what you said?

J: Mary and my mother and father went to Houston. She told me when, I guess pretty much right away after they had gone over there, but I didn't know what was going on. I didn't follow up on it. I didn't ask her anything about it. Now, all this time is passing, and it dawned on me.

TH: Yeah, yeah. You remembered it. What prompted you to go with his Mom and Dad?

M: Because it was in the community, you know, from old friends of the family, they knew the family from way back, that was some of the things that her grandmother . . .

TH: Her grandmother? Sandy's grandmother?

M: Uh-huh. Her grandmother is the one who reared her.

TH: I see.

M: And so she had a lot of control over her. It was being rumoured that was what was going on in their situation. . . .

TH: In their?

M: James and Sandy.

TH: Okay. That was going on—that somehow grandma, as she had controlled Sandy, Sandy was trying to control . . . .

M: Uh-huh. Him also.

TH: Okay. I got you.

M: And she was noted for controlling her husband. And James's mother and father were aware of the situation, plus they had informed me, they had advised James, because of the lifestyle and the things that they knew about the family, the grandmother and all, from years back, not to get into the family. That he would be "eatup". And I think that's one reason he was mad at his mother, was because she called it. Not be able to handle the type of situation. So, my cousin over in the Houston area and I are very close. So we were talking about the situation, and she knew this lady over there that she felt like from knowing her that she could sight one of these things had taken place. So she did. She talked to the lady and the lady gave me a call. And she asked me to send her a quarter in the mail. To hold it in my hand and send it to her, and then that's when she called me. And uh, she asked me to come over there. And she told me to be careful, because Sandy was trying to do the same thing to me, because James was definitely under her power.

TH: Gosh, that's amazing. So you went over with his mom and dad, and she told you to be careful, and once you got there, what did she advise you?

M: Well, she told me that James didn't need to be anywhere near Sandy. She didn't need to have anything to do with his food, any type of his possessions, anything. As long as she was . . .

Comment: Here we find similar advice to what the therapist had given regarding breaking the spell.

TH: Like a bedroom set?

M: As long as (everybody starts laughing) . . .

TH: Go ahead. I didn't mean to interrupt you.

M: As long as she was nearby, and he was close to her, she would be in full control of his life. He would . . . She wanted to say that his sickness, it appeared like that, but it wasn't a really mental condition.

TH: Man, this just blows my mind. Okay, so what did you do with that knowledge?

M: I told him about it. And she asked me to go to New Orleans. I thought it was silly, but I did it.

TH: Why New Orleans?

M: Marie Laveaux, the famous voodoo queen, is buried there. For both of us to go.

J: I went with her.

TH: To go to Marie Laveaux?

J: No, no . . .

M: She's been dead for years. To go to her grave. And touch her tomb. And James, he was supposed to mark something on her tomb, but he was not supposed to go back near Sandy, but he did.

TH: As a way of breaking the spell. Because the woman was . . . her magic was so strong . . . her voodoo queen. There's a song about her. Listen, I need to ask you a question. Are you actively involved in religion, or do you go to church in any way?

M: Yeah.

TH: Which?

M: Protestant.

TH: Both of you are Protestant? Both of you go to church regularly, fairly regularly, or . . .

M: For the last six months, we haven't been going regular like we should have, you know—oversleep.

J: And the reason that is . . . has been all along, Wendel, is that Joey gets up early except on Sunday. And I get up early, well, not early, but well in time to get everybody up and go to church. Joey will not wake up on purpose, because he doesn't want to get up and go to church anyway.

M: And he's in on it.

J: No. It just seems like it. But I haven't been waking up lately either. I've just been . . .

TH: Have you tried using your faith in any way to battle this situation with Sandy?

M: Uh-huh.

TH: Tell me about that.

M: Well I guess with our minister's assistance from our church, you've probably seen some articles in the paper—the Reverend Lynn, he's suppose to be ... well ... blessed with the healing.

TH: He has healing power?

M: Uh, we've been advised, at least I have, to pray, and certain scriptures to read. For anything, not only for her. And so, James had me believing some of the things he says sometimes.

ACT II: CREATING THE RESOURCEFUL CONTEXT

TH: Okay, so say eleven. No, more than eleven or twelve years ago, you were given some advice from this healer. I don't know who she was, but I think it was utterly sound advice and if you had followed it, you would have never met me, and you probably would have never ended up in that hospital. The advice was, and this is a quote, you said, "She said you were not to see Sandy, you were not to have any possessions of Sandy's, nothing of hers, no food that Sandy cooked for you". Right? And uh, that is it. We have agreed with this healer. In a way, you have been possessed by this trance or spell, and the spell's got to be broken before anything else. This has got to come first. Now, the kind of bickering, for lack of a better word, that you two get into where Mary feels like you don't ask her opinion of things, or you may feel like he's not accessible to you, you know, when you try to talk to him, that's part of this. You are frozen by this thing ... by this spell. In fact, I don't want to get into this in depth, but even some of the team are of the mind that this spell is so strong that it has even affected your going to church. You know, Mary, for a long time, you were the one who was up on Sundays and you were ready to go. Now you are laying in the bed, and you [James] are up. It is such a powerful spell that it has got to be broken, and the only way you're going to break this spell is by getting rid of those possessions—whatever they happen to be. For example, not only your bedroom set which, I think, that's just got to go. And if Sandy ever gave you—for example, you remember one time you mentioned old clothes that James sometimes would put on? Right? I'm suspecting that Sandy might have even helped him buy those clothes.

M: She probably did.

Comment: Given the family history with respect to voodoo, the previously constructed resourceful context is further maintained and solidified. This enables the therapist to return the couple to the task at hand: getting rid of the bedroom furniture.

ACT III: PRESCRIPTION FOR ENACTING THE RESOURCEFUL CONTEXT

TH: And if it's anything that Sandy's involved in buying, it has got to go. Because as the healer told you long ago, the woman from Houston, she said, aside from going to Marie Laveaux's grave, she said that your advice is not to see Sandy, don't take anything of Sandy's, no possessions of Sandy's, no food from Sandy . . . I think this healer was on to something.

J: Well you might be. You think around that house, the gifts I have . . . the pitcher and bowl in the bedroom, they gave us that. And that thing, you know, on the wall, didn't they give us that?

M: Those are things supposedly that the children gave us.

TH: The children are one thing, but if it is from Sandy, that's an entirely different thing.

M: He's talking about these things that you don't want to part with. Uh, like these old clothes . . .

TH: I'm talking about anything that Sandy had a hand in putting in your hands. And if you're the sort that can't bear . . . now this is me talking, this isn't the team . . . destroying something that's valuable, give it to Goodwill [a charity organization]. My point is, to get it out of the house. And you two have got to do something.

M: Well, I think that's part of the thing with the bedroom set.

TH: It's nice, yeah. But look what's it has been doing to you for ten years. I am convinced of this.

J: I agree. I agree.

TH: And when you get back home and if the two of you can't come to an agreement about what you're going to do about it, that's just a comment about how strong this spell is, because I don't care how nice it is, if it's causing this kind of misery where you can't even get together . . .

J: What Mary's saying, she thinks that I'm too attached to it. I feel it's too nice to get rid of. But that . . . under these circumstances, that's probably not the case. (Turning to Mary) Don't you feel that I'm too attached, because if you're thinking like that, just don't think like that.

TH: What could you do to demonstrate that, James? To demonstrate that you're not that attached.

J: If I do like you said all along, start hauling it out of there, then that would let her know how I feel about it.

M: If you . . .

J: See, she's still hung up on "If I would do that".

M: Let me tell you why, Wendel. These old clothes that he pulls out, in one group, it was ridiculous. Every time he would get in an uproar, he would put these things on. And when we'd see these clothes, we knew.

TH: You see, I will bet you money that those clothes were bought when he was with Sandy.

M: Yeah, they were.

TH: And man. I'm telling you what, the facts are the facts, you guys have been in suspended animation.

M: Some of those clothes, I did manage to get them out of the house while was in the hospital—the first time he went to the hospital. And he brings that back to me. "What happened to my clothes, you'd better go get them. Right now!"

J: These shirts, in particular, and there were some shoes and things, but those shirts were more like entertainer shirts. Like James Brown, and so on.

TH: You know what Brad told me one time? Just a few minutes ago, we were talking about how certain witch doctors had such powers that they would put a hex on the front door of a person's house, and they walked through the door the voodoo would be put on them in that way. So as you talk about shoes and stuff—look, if it was Sandy that gave it to you, it has got to go. Listen, you are not to see her, you're not to keep any possessions that she gave you or jointly to both of you. No food, nothing.

J: Well, uh . . .

CN: I just want to come in here. My voice is weak, but my message is strong.

TH: She probably put the voodoo on your voice.

CN: True, but there's two others back there [team members] who have lost their voices too. There is one thing that was said that is so important that it knocked us out of our seats and I'm here just to add my voice to the strength of Wendel's voice. Which is, and I don't know whether you folks believe in voodoo or if you believe in spirits or if you believe in faith, but there's something going here that allows people from ten years ago and others now to say get that stuff out. And that it does have some kind of hold on you. It's holding your life up and right now is a critical time because we all know what's going on, the spell's going to get tighter. So now is the time to act. We talked about you folks going home right now, right this minute, and when you get home, we're going to sit here and wait for you, you call us and say "we're home" and you tell us what you're going to do to get rid of that stuff right now. That way we can be here as a little extra strength . . .

TH: To help you break this spell.

CN: See, I have a hunch, part of that going to New Orleans to see the grave of Marie Laveaux was to give you a little strength to be able to say no to this hex. You didn't have the strength, because you didn't go, did you?

J: We went.

CN: Did you feel the strength?

J: Well, I'll tell you. We weren't married then, I was kind of . . . I don't even know if I was divorced, was I?

M: No.

J: That was kind of when everything was just dragging.

CN: That was because you didn't believe that this thing could hold you for ten years.

TH: You couldn't believe it.

CN: See, I think that you need to get it out. You have to get it out. Go home. Could you guys do that? Could you do that?

TH: Then call us.

CN: We are going to stop everything. We're going to freeze our time and we're going to sit here and wait. And you call us and let us know how you are doing.

TH: Go in the bedroom, then call and tell us what it is you're doing.

J: Okay, that's fine.

TH: And don't let Sandy get the two of you at odds with each other, so that you don't carry this out, if you understand what I'm saying. Because if there's anything to this, it is priority one. It's got to happen.

M: You say the whole bedroom set today or just one piece?

TH: I'm saying it is time take action.

J: Okay, let me tell you what I'm going to do. I'm going to get home and I'll call before we do anything. I'm going to narrow down some clothing out of my closet. But I'm not going to have you hold before we even get started.

TH: And tell us what you're about to get . . . because if you stick to what we had said . . . is that you're going to burn it and keep the ashes.

CN: Let's get going.

TH: Oh listen, by the way . . .

J: You can keep the lighter, okay? (lighting a cigarette, then handing the lighter to Wendel)

TH: Thanks, James.

CN: I would like to suggest that you two only discuss what you're
     going to do when you get home because it's going to be easy
     to drift into talking about other things, because it's close to
     lunch . . .

J: I know, I know. Because she is going to start talking about
     how much work she's got to do in her job . . . but I'm going to
     the closet and I'm going to take care of that. Ain't nothing in
     her closet . . .

TH: Okay. But don't you hesitate, because that'll signal to her that
     you don't want to.

J: I think that's what she's thinking right now. That I'm attached
     to this.

WR: But you're going to show her.

J: It's time for action. No more lip-service.

CASE FOLLOW-UP

During the two weeks after this session, James and Mary gradually
removed each piece of the bedroom set left to James by Sandy during the divorce settlement, burning them one by one in the fireplace.
During the past six months they report having had very little con-
tact with Sandy. In sessions, which were held monthly, Mary and
James became more spontaneous with each other and described a
steady improvement in their relationship. James has not returned to
the hospital for more than two years. He has enrolled in an intro-
ductory counseling class at a local university.

CHAPTER SEVEN

Training exercises for developing the therapist's creativity and resourcefulness

Bradford P. Keeney & Wendel A. Ray

We have used the following exercises to help therapists practice and develop rhetorical skills and therapeutic strategies. All of these exercises encourage therapists to utilize their imagination and creativity. When practicing these exercises therapists should not worry about whether their responses are clinically sound, safe, appropriate, or even ethical. These exercises are for helping to loosen the therapist's attachment to clichés, recipes, and routine ways of being in a session. Like the exercises conducted in a school of performing arts, therapists should free themselves to practice exercising their inventiveness. Following the practice of an exercise, therapists may analyse, critique, and dialogue about the utterances that came forth.

We have used these exercises in a variety of training settings, including graduate course work, postgraduate clinical training programs, and workshops. The exercises are not a substitute for training. We regard live supervision of clinical casework to be the most important learning structure for training therapists. These exercises are a supplement to training that aim to help liberate and expand the therapist's imagination and choices of conduct. They are presented in skeletal form so that therapists may more easily modify and use these exercises in any way that may help the bringing forth of resourcefulness in therapy.

"Getting Unstuck"

1. Break into groups of 3–5 people and come up with several examples of how therapists get stuck in their work. For example, particular ways of getting stuck to an idea, belief, technique, orientation, and so forth, can be elaborated.

2. Come up with an intervention that addresses each example of being stuck.

3. Share findings with other groups.

4. Choose several examples with interventions to be performed as a simulated session in front of the whole training class.

"Creating Lines for Client Provocations"

1. Make a list of possible utterances from clients that make you squirm or uncertain as to what you would say. For instance:

   "I'm not sure therapy is doing me any good."

   "I thought about killing myself."

   "I don't know if you can help me."

2. For each client provocation, create at least five different therapeutic comeback lines.

"Creating a Case Dialogue"

1. Have the entire group break into two lines of chairs, facing one another. One line of trainees is to assume the voice of "the client" while the other line of trainees assumes "the therapist's" voice.

2. Any person in the client line may say only one line. The next line must come from a person in the therapist line. And so on, back and forth, in a fashion that creates a therapeutic conversation. The person who offers a line must wait in silence until after another person in his or her line has uttered a subsequent line.

3. All members of a line are to listen to the voices of their line as the voice of one person. One whole line is a whole client and another whole line is a whole therapist.

"Talking with Meaningful Noise: Creating Theory"

1. Have the group put on a blackboard a list of metaphors that indicate the most important key terms used to understand therapeutic change.
2. Members are then to create theoretic sentences and generalizations by stringing together any of the above derived terms. No other words can be used other than "the", "if", "an", "and", and so forth.

"Creating Hypnotic/Trance Injunctions"

1. The group is to make a list of metaphors associated with hypnotic experience.
2. Create strings of sentences, sensical and/or nonsensical, that connect these metaphors together. Say them as if they were trance injunctions.

"Imagining the Impossible as Possible"

1. Each person is to create a line, intervention, or explanation that one could never imagine saying to a client. It may be considered impossible because one thinks it is too wild, dangerous, uncomfortable, or whatever.
2. The group then invents an imaginary case story that demonstrates how that "impossible" line or intervention would make sense and be resourceful in the context of the invented case story.

"Imagining the Safe Therapeutic Line as Dangerous"

1. Each person is to create a list of three "safe" therapeutic lines. For instance:

"How are you today?"

"I understand what you mean."

"Take a day off for yourself."

2. The group then creates clinical case stories demonstrating how these "safe" lines may be dangerous in a particular context.

"Therapy for Movie Scenes"

1. Each group finds a 1–5 minute excerpt from a popular movie that is a clear set-up or Act I. It does not have to be the beginning of a movie. What is important is that it is an excerpt that does not require that the observer previously have seen the whole film. The excerpt on its own presents a clearly defined problematic situation implying the need for resolution.

2. The group then creates an imaginary middle and final scene that resolves the problem.

"Making Connections"

1. The class divides itself into three groups who go to separate places to conduct different tasks.

2. The first group invents five minutes of a hypothetical conversation in the beginning of therapy. The second group invents an intervention not designed for any particular situation. (Note: The second group has no awareness of the first group's conversation.)

3. All three groups come together and the first group enacts the therapeutic conversation. Following that conversation, the second group acts as a consultant and says the following, "we want you to do the following task. We'll present it to you and let you think about it while we go take a short consultation break. We'll then send someone in to explain the task." The second group then presents the intervention they had invented.

4. The third group leaves the room and invents some way of connecting the intervention to the conversation so that it has meaning. When this is done, they return and present it to the whole group.

Creating "LIST"

When clinicians talk to one another in a training context, it may be important to note that there are those occasions where talk is focused more upon theory, while other times it is focused more upon practice. We help trainees manage clinical information by a heuristic that orders descriptions of therapy into four categories:

L: Lines
I: Intervention
S: Strategy
T: Theory

This acronym, LIST, provides an efficient way of organizing talk about the clinical situation in a way that is conducive to the practice of RFT. In a group setting students are encouraged to practise recognizing when someone is talking about a specific therapeutic line (i.e. the specific words that are spoken) and when one is articulating an understanding of theory. They also practise identifying talk concerned with creating a strategy aimed at moving clients from Act I (an impoverishing conversation) into Act II (towards a more resourceful conversation). And, finally, they practise identifying and creating talk that aspires to provide an intervention for enacting a resourceful context.

"Using a Storyboard in Therapy"

1. Simulate a clinical session where there are clients, a therapist, and a story-keeper.
2. The story-keeper uses a blackboard or poster board to keep track of the flow of conversation in therapy. He or she may interrupt at any time to ask clarifying questions such as:

"What's the opening chapter?"

"Who are the main characters?"

"When did this story begin?"

"Can we move into the next chapter?"

"Did you just go back to the introduction again?"

Note that the story-keeper is really a co-therapist but does not explicitly assume that role. He or she acts more like a reporter who only asks questions to help keep the story clear.

"Fortune Cookie Therapy"

1. A group of trainees write twelve questions or statements from the perspective of the client on index cards (one sentence per card). Those are then placed in a bowl.

2. A therapy case simulation is enacted using other trainees who have no knowledge of what the cards state. At any moment, the client performers may reach into the bowl and randomly select a client card with a question or statement on it. This is then uttered as if it were part of the on-going conversation.

3. The procedure may be reversed, where the twelve cards are statements/questions written from the perspective of the therapist's voice.

"How To Learn a Style of Therapy: Part One"

1. Choose a classic case study that is inspiring to you. The case may be transcribed in a published book or available as a training tape.

2. Memorize the whole case.

3. Perform the case and assume the voices of all characters. Set up different chairs and move from chair to chair in order to enact the whole session.

4. When you have mastered a particular therapy session, try improvising on it.

"How to Learn a Style of Therapy: Part Two"

1. Perform an imaginary session of a particular school of therapy, expressing all the voices of all characters—clients and therapist.

2. Perform an imaginary session where you are the therapist and the client (another trainee) says the "right lines," that is, the statements that help you bring forth the kind of therapy you are trying to enact.

3. Perform an imaginary session where you are the therapist, and the client (another trainee) occasionally makes it difficult for you to conduct the particular style of therapy you desire. For instance, in the case of trying to perform a problem-solving therapy:

Therapist: "What's the problem?"

Client: "I don't want to discuss problems. I want you to empathize with my feelings."

"Creating an Exercise"

1. In a group situation, choose three readers to enact the conversation that follows. One reader is the narrator, another a woman therapist, and the third a male therapist.

Narrator: The following is an exercise created to help free therapists from psychotherapy clichés and scripted ways of performing. The session begins nowhere in particular and aims to go nowhere in general. Are you ready?

Man: Are you ready?

Woman: Yes, let's begin.

Man: Let's see if I have this right. We're suppose to look like we're reading a script, when in fact there are no words written on the pages we hold in front of us.

Woman: Well there are no words in front of me, but I don't know whether you have a script. One of the rules of this encounter is that we can't look at each other's script.

Man: Whatever the case, we are each to pretend that we're reading lines from a script without knowing whether the other person has a script or not.

Woman: Isn't that deceptive?

Man: Is it less deceptive than therapists who speak memorized scripts to their clients, but pretend they are not?

Woman: I see what we're doing. We're turning therapy upside down. Remember what was said about most therapy being a collection of about a dozen clichés, and that what most therapists do is dispense these clichés into conversations.

Man: Well-worn lines like,
      "I hear you saying that," or
      "How do you feel about that?" or
      "Who's closest to Mom in this family?" or
      "What have you tried as a solution?"

Woman: So how is this conversation going to help free us to think up other lines?

Man: I'm not sure that's what this conversation is about. Maybe there is no purpose to this encounter.

Woman: How do you feel about that?

Man: If your family were here, who in your family would be most likely to ask that question?

Woman: I hear what you're saying.

Man: So what's the problem we want to address?

Woman: I think the issue is how to say something other than therapy clichés.

Man: Let's call in our consultant for advice.

2. The group then creates the rest of the script, one line at a time. One way of doing this is to have every trainee write one line that is not a boring cliché about therapy. A line is read and then the group adds conversation to weave it into the text. Consider creating an ending to the conversation that includes a story of how this exercise became a part of this book.

CHAPTER EIGHT

After words

As the premises and methods described in the first two chapters and the subsequent case studies have demonstrated, RFT, while rooted in the same traditions as Brief Therapy, represents a radical departure from other brief therapy orientations. Rather than focusing on attempted solutions as is done in problem-focused approaches, expanding upon existing solutions as in solution-focused models, or focusing upon the social contextualization of the problem as in the Milan Systemic orientation, RFT moves completely away from talking about problems as quickly as possible within the logic of the therapeutic conversation. *Any* potentially resourceful line presented by the client or therapist is expanded upon and utilized to create resourceful contexts for action. Therapy becomes a process of maintaining the more resourceful context.

We invite readers to experiment with RFT in their own clinical work, supervision, and training, and we close with a few quotations we have found resourceful.

* * *

* "That's kind of normal, isn't it?"
  – Don Jackson

* "One thing leads to another."
  – John Weakland

* "We are all more simply human than anything else."
  – Harry Stack Sullivan

* "When did you settle on this as being the best explanation?"
  – Gianfranco Cecchin

* "Don't bite my finger, look where I'm pointing."
  – Warren McCulloch

* "How crazy a particular person appears to you depends on your own frame of reference and your own experience."
  – Don D. Jackson

* "Do not hold any belief except as a working hypothesis to be discarded as soon as possible."
  – Warren S. McCulloch

* "The thing to do is to get your patient, any way you wish, any way you can, to do something."
  – Milton H. Erickson

* "If it ain't broke, don't fix it."
  – Anonymous

* "Too often psychotherapists try to deal with their patients by using their doctoral degree language, trying to explain the ego, superego, and the id, conscious and unconscious, and the patient doesn't know whether you're talking about corn, potatoes, or hash. Therefore, you try to use the language of the patient."
  – Milton H. Erickson.

* This playfulness is the product of the shared ability to appreciate the power of redescribing, the power of language to make new and different things possible and important—an appreciation which becomes possible only when one's aim becomes an expanding repertoire of alternative descriptions rather than The One Right Description."
  – Richard Rorty

* "It's unverifiable, so you can't say it's not true."
  – Anonymous

* "It takes two to know one."
  – Gregory Bateson

* "May God keep us from single vision and Newton's sleep!"
  – William Blake

* "The Laws of Nature become inventions, rigor is married to imagination, and Nature is fiction, made up by us acting together. Ultimately this means seeing oneself through the eyes of the other."
  – Heinz Von Foerster

* "There is no 'not caring' . . . [we are] only *relatively* independent."
  – Don D. Jackson

* "What's the problem?"
  – Wyatt Earp

* "Is there a miracle in your life?"
  – Oral Roberts

* "The statement is pointless. The finger is speechless."
  – R.D. Laing

* "God save us from what man does in the name of good."
  – Paladin

* "Words are action."
  – RFT

* "Actions are cleaner than words."
  – RFT

* "Silence is a noisy act."
  – RFT

* "Uncommon sense often makes better sense."
  – RFT

* "Typically, the more you ask, the more lost you get."
  – RFT

* "More information is less."
  – RFT

* "Act in order to hear."
  – RFT

* "When your job is done, stop."
  – RFT

* "The end."
  – Shakespeare

REFERENCES AND BIBLIOGRAPHY

Bateson, G. (1972). *Steps to an Ecology of Mind*. New York: Jason Aronson.

Bateson, G., Jackson, D., Haley, J., & Weakland, J. (1956). Toward a theory of schizophrenia. *Behavioral Science, 1* (4): 251–264.

Boscolo, L., Cecchin, G., Hoffman, L., & Penn, P. (1987). *Milan Systemic Family Therapy*. New York: Basic Books.

Cecchin, G., Lane, G., & Ray, W. (1991). Vom strategischen Vorgehen zur Nicht-intervention. *Familien Dynamik, 17* (1): 3–18.

Cecchin, G., Lane, G., & Ray, W. (1992). *Irreverence: A Strategy for Therapists' Survival*. London: Karnac Books.

Cecchin, G., Lane, G., & Ray, W. (1993). From strategizing to non-intervention. *Journal of Marital & Family Therapy, 19*: 125–136.

de Shazer, S. (1982). *Patterns of Brief Family Therapy: An Ecosystemic Approach*. New York: Guilford Press.

de Shazer, S. (1988). *Clues: Investigating Solutions in Brief Therapy*. New York: W. W. Norton.

Erickson, M. (1980). *The Collected Papers of Milton H. Erickson, M.D.*, Vols. 1–4, edited by E. Rossi. New York: Irvington.

Erickson, M. (1985). *Life Reframing in Hypnosis*. New York: Irvington.

Erickson, M., Haley, J., & Weakland, J. (1959). A transcript of a trance induction with commentary. *American Journal of Clinical Hypnosis* (October): 49–84.

Fisch, R., Weakland, J., & Segal, L. (1982). *The Tactics of Change: Doing Therapy Briefly.* San Francisco, CA: Jossey-Bass.

Goffman, E. (1961). *Asylums: Essays on the Social Situation of Mental Patients and Other Inmates.* New York: Anchor Books.

Haley, J. (Ed.) (1967). *Advanced Techniques of Hypnosis and Therapy: Selected Papers of Milton H. Erickson.* New York: Grune & Stratton.

Haley, J. (1973). *Uncommon Therapy: The Psychiatric Techniques of Milton H. Erickson, MD.* New York: W. W. Norton.

Haley, J. (1976). *Problem-Solving Therapy.* San Francisco, CA: Jossey-Bass.

Jackson, D. (1965). The study of the family. *Family Process, 4:* 1–20.

Jackson, D. (1967a). Schizophrenia: The nosological nexus. *Excerpta Medica International Congress Series, 151:* 111–120. Also in P. Watzlawick & J. Weakland (Eds.), *The Interactional View* (pp. 193–208). New York: W. W. Norton.

Jackson, D. (1967b). The fear of change. *Medical Opinion and Review, 3* (3): 34–41.

Jackson, D. (1967c). The myth of normality. *Medical Opinion and Review, 3* (5): 28–33.

Jackson, D. (1967d). *Family Therapy with a "Schizophrenic" Young Adult and his Parents* [Uncirculated film]. Palo Alto, CA: MRI.

Jackson, D., & Weakland, J. (1959). Schizophrenic symptoms and family interaction. *Archives of General Psychiatry, 1:* 618–621.

Jackson, D., & Weakland, J. (1961). Conjoint family therapy. *Psychiatry, 24* (Suppl. #2): 30–45.

Keeney, B. (1983). *Aesthetics of Change.* New York: Guilford Press.

Keeney, B. (1991). *Improvisational Therapy: A Practical Guide for Creative Clinical Strategies.* New York: Guilford Press.

Keeney, B., & Ray, W. (1992a). Kicking research in the ass: Provocations for reform. *AFTA News Journal, 47:* 67–68.

Keeney, B., & Ray, W. (1992b). Shifting from supervision to super-audition. *AAMFT Supervision Bulletin, 5* (2): 3.

Keeney, B., & Ross, J. (1992). *Mind in Therapy: Constructing Systemic Family Therapies.* Pretoria, South Africa: University of South Africa, Sigma Press.

Keeney, B., & Silverstein, O. (1987). *The Therapeutic Voice of Olga Silverstein.* New York: Guilford Press.

Miller, J. (1989). Wonder as hinge. *International Philosophical Quarterly,* *29* (1): 44–66.

Mullahy, P. (1967). *A Study of Interpersonal Relations.* New York: Science House.

Palazzoli, M., Cecchin, G., Boscolo, L., & Prata, G. (1978a). Hypothesizing–circularity–neutrality. *Family Process, 19:* 3–12

Palazzoli, M., Cecchin, G., Boscolo, L., & Prata, G. (1978b). *Paradox and Counterparadox.* New York: Jason Aronson.

Ray, W. (1990). Die interaktionale Therapie von Don D. Jackson. *Zeitschrift fur Systemische Therapie* (January): 5–30

Ray, W. (1992a). Family therapy of adolescent substance abuse. *Louisiana Journal of Counseling & Development, 3* (1): 8–15.

Ray, W. (1992b). Our future in the past: Lessons from Don Jackson for practicing family therapy with hospitalized adolescents, *Family Therapy, 19:* 61–72.

Ray, W. (1993). John Weakland: An appreciation. *AAMFT News, 24* (1): 27–28.

Ray, W. Keeney, B., Parker, K., & Pascal, D. (1992). The invisible wall: A method for breaking a relations impasse. *Louisiana Journal of Counseling and Development, 3* (1): 32–35.

Ray, W., & Saxon, W. (1992). Nonconfrontive use of video playback in brief family therapy. *Journal of Marital and Family Therapy, 18:* 63–70.

Sullivan, H. S. (1953). *Collected Works.* New York: W. W. Norton.

Stanton, A., & Schwartz, M. (1954). *The Mental Hospital.* New York: Basic Books.

Tannenbaum, F. (1938). The dramatization of evil. *Crime & Punishment* (pp. 19–20). New York: Columbia University Press.

von Foerster, H. (1984a). *Cybernetics of Cybernetics.* Urbana, IL: Biological Computer Laboratory.

von Foerster, H. (1984b). *Observing Systems.* Seaside, CA: Intersystems Press.

Watzlawick, P., Beavin, J., & Jackson, D. (1967). *Pragmatics of Human Communication.* New York: W. W. Norton.

Watzlawick, P., Weakland, J., & Fisch, R. (1974). *Change: Principles of Problem Formation and Problem Resolution.* New York: W. W. Norton.

Weakland, J. (1967). Communication and behavior—An introduction. *American Behavioral Scientist, 10* (8, Special issue—J. Weakland, Guest Editor): 1–4.

Weakland, J. (1969). Anthropology, psychiatry, and communication. *American Anthropologist, 71* (5): 880–888.

Weakland, J. (1983). Family therapy with individuals. *Journal of Systemic and Strategic Therapies*, 2 (4): 1–9.

Weakland, J., Fisch, R., Watzlawick, P., & Bodin, A. (1974). Brief therapy: Focused problem resolution. *Family Process* 13: 141–168.

Weakland, J., & Ray, W. (Eds.) (in press). *Propagations: 30 Years of MRI Influence*. New York: Haworth.

ABOUT THE AUTHORS

Wendel A. Ray, MSW, Ph.D., is Associate Professor of Marriage and Family Therapy at Northeast Louisiana University in Monroe; a Research Associate and Director of the Don D. Jackson Archive at the Mental Research Institute, Palo Alto, California. Author and co-author of numerous articles and book chapters on interactionally oriented brief therapy, he is co-author of three other books: *Irreverence: A Strategy for Therapists' Survival* (1992), with Gianfranco Cecchin and Gerry Lane, *Propagations: 30 Years of M.R.I. Influence* (in press), co-edited with John H. Weakland, and *The Cybernetics of Prejudices: Prejudice and Accountability in Therapy*, with Gianfranco Cecchin and Gerry Lane (in press). A clinical member and approved supervisor of the American Association for Marriage and Family Therapy, he is currently President of the Louisiana Association for Marriage and Family Therapy.

Bradford P. Keeney, Ph.D., is presently Professor and Director of Scholarly Studies, Graduate Programs in Professional Psychology, University of St. Thomas. He was the former director of several doctoral programs in family therapy and has worked at the

Ackerman Institute for Family Therapy in New York City, the Philadelphia Child Guidance Clinic, and the Menninger Foundation. A clinical member, approved supervisor, and fellow of the American Association for Marriage and Family Therapy, he is author of over eleven books and has lectured throughout the world. In addition to his therapeutic and academic activities, he is a jazz pianist and composer.

DATE DUE

DEMCO 38-297